# *Nita Mehta's*
## VEGETARIAN
# Chinese COOKING

# *Nita Mehta's*

## VEGETARIAN

 # Chinese

## COOKING

including the latest Chinese dishes that you enjoy at
Chinese restaurants!

# *Nita Mehta*

B.Sc. (Home Science), M.Sc. (Food and Nutrition)
Gold Medalist

## Tanya Mehta

**SNAB**
Publishers Pvt. Ltd.

## *Nita Mehta's*
### VEGETARIAN
# 🐉 Chinese 🐉
### COOKING

© Copyright 2003 **SNAB🌏** Publishers Pvt Ltd

First Hard bound Edition 2003

ISBN 81-7869-058-6

*Food Styling & Photography:* **SNAB🌏**

*Layout and laser typesetting:*

National Information
Technology Academy
3A/3, Asaf Ali Road
New Delhi-110002
☎ 23252948

*Published by:*

**Publishers Pvt Ltd**
**3A/3 Asaf Ali Road**
**New Delhi-110002**

*The Best of*
*Cookery*
*Books*

*Editorial and Marketing office:*
**E-348, Greater Kailash-II, N.Delhi-48**
*Fax:*91-11-6235218 *Tel:*91-11-6214011, 6238727
*E-Mail:* nitamehta@email.com
        snab@snabindia.com

*Website:* http://www.nitamehta.com
*Website:* http://www.snabindia.com

*Picture on cover:* **Potato Strings in Hot Ginger Sauce**

*Picture on page 2-3:* **Honey Rice Balls**
**Broccoli in Garlic Butter Sauce**

*Picture on page 4:* **Hoisin Stir Fry Okra**

*Picture on page 129:* **Corn Rolls, Honey Crispies**

*Printed at:*
INTERNATIONAL PRINT-O-PAC LTD

*Distributed by:*
THE VARIETY BOOK DEPOT
A.V.G. Bhavan, M 3 Con Circus
New Delhi - 110 001
Tel: 23417175, 23412567; Fax: 23415335

## Price: Rs. 245/-

# Introduction

"Vegetarian Chinese Cooking" includes the classic traditional recipes as well as the new Chinese dishes now available at good Chinese eateries.

Chinese food is full of flavour and the texture of vegetables in every dish is crisp. Keeping this in mind, the recipes have been put down in a very orderly manner, so as to retain the colour and crispiness of vegetables. The correct cutting of vegetables which exposes the maximum surface area of the vegetable, helps make cooking faster, which in turn keeps the vegetable crunchy. A special chapter on techniques of vegetable cutting and cooking is thus included.

The specialty starter "Dim Sums" with a special dipping sauce will set the mood rolling for the party. Follow it up with a light thin soup like "Lemon Coriander Soup" which whets the appetite rather than killing it as some of the heavy soups can be blamed for!

The main course has lots to offer. Our favourite Paneer or Tofu in a special Fennel flavoured Sauce and the Stir Fried Okra in Hoisin Sauce will make a perfect meal with Pepper Fried Rice and Pea Cinnamon Noodles.

Honey Crispies served with ice cream at the end of the meal will leave your guests in awe of you and waiting for the next invitation. So, how about a complete Chinese layout for your friends and family for the forthcoming dinner party!

Enjoy the taste of China, all cooked in a simple delicious manner.

*Nita Mehta*

# ABOUT THE RECIPES

## WHAT'S IN A CUP?

**INDIAN CUP**
1 teacup = 200 ml liquid
**AMERICAN CUP**
1 cup = 240 ml liquid (8 oz)
**The recipes in this book were tested with the Indian teacup which holds 200 ml liquid.**

# Contents

## SOUPS    36

# VEGETABLE DISHES    53

### Important Tips...    53
### Techniques of Cutting Vegetables    54
### Techniques of Chinese Cooking    55

# RICE & NOODLES 102

# DESSERTS 122

# Ingredients used for Chinese Dishes

**Bean Sprouts:** These are shoots of moong beans or soya beans. The texture is crisp. Bean sprouts are a rich source of vitamins and minerals. To make bean sprouts at home, soak ½ cup of green beans (saboot moong dal) for about 8 hours. Discard water and tie in a muslin cloth. Keep them tied for 2-3 days, remembering to wet the cloth each day. When the shoots are long enough, wash carefully in water. Fresh bean sprouts will keep for several days if refrigerated in a perforated plastic bag.

**Chilli Sauce:** This is a hot, spicy and tangy sauce made from chillies and vinegar.

**Chinese Wine:** There are many kinds of wine made from rice. Chinese wine can be substituted by ordinary dry sherry.

**Agar-Agar:** This is a dried seaweed. The white fibrous strands require soaking and are used like gelatine. It is used for puddings and as a setting agent.

**Cornflour:** This is used to thicken sauces. Dissolve some cornflour in little water to make a paste and add it to the boiling liquid. Remember to stir the sauce continuously, when the cornflour paste is being added.

**Ajinomoto (Monosodium Glutamate):** A white crystalline substance commonly known as MSG. It is used in Chinese cookery for enhancing the flavour of dishes.

**Mushrooms:** There are many varieties which are used in Chinese cooking. To prepare dried mushrooms for cooking, soak them in hot water for ½ hour to soften. Discard any hard stems.

**Snow Peas:** These are from the pea family and are used in cooking just like we use French beans. These are threaded like French beans and the whole pod is edible. Snap off the stem end of pea pod and pull the string across the pea pod to remove it.

**Bamboo Shoots:** Fresh tender shoots of bamboo plant are available rarely, but tinned bamboo shoots are easily available in the big stores.

**Bok Choy:** Bok choy is a variety of Chinese cabbage and is also known as spoon cabbage because the leaves are spoon shaped. This plant has dark green leaves with a white stalk and is an excellent vegetable for stir frying. Both the stalk and the leaves can be used.

**Bean Curd or Tofu:** Bean Curd or Tofu is prepared from soya bean milk and resembles the Indian Paneer in taste and looks. I have thus substituted it with paneer to give you a few exciting delicacies.

**Noodles:** Coiled noodles (nest type) called chow are available in small packets in the market or with the vegetable vendors. These are preferred to straight ones. They are usually cooked in boiling water till just done for about 2 minutes only. Never overcook noodles as they turn thick on over cooking.

**Rice Noodles:** These extremely thin noodles resemble long, transculent white hair. Rice noodles are just soaked in hot water for 10 minutes and then drained before use. When deep fried they explode dramatically into a tangle of airy, crunchy strands that are used for garnish.

**Sesame Oil:** An aromatic oil produced from sesame seeds *(til ka tel)*. Adds flavour to dips, sauces, salads and soups.

**Soya Sauce:** There are two kinds. One is dark and the other is light. Both are used for flavouring soups, stir fried dishes and for seasoning all Chinese foods.

**Spring Onions:** These are sometimes called scallions or green onions. In absence of it you can substitute it with regular onion. The green part is also used and should be added at the end.

**Vinegar:** Chinese vinegars are made from fermented rice.

**Five Spice Powder:** This mixture of five ground spices is slightly sweet and pungent. Roast together 2 tsp peppercorns (saboot kali mirch), 3 star anise (phool chakri), 6 laung (cloves), 6" stick dalchini (cinnamon), 3 tsp saunf (fennel). Grind all the ingredients of the powder in a small mixer to a powder. Strain the powder through a sieve (channi).

**Seasoning Cube and Vegetable Stock:** Vegetable stock is an important agent for most Chinese soup and sauces. However, if you do not have stock ready or feel lazy to make a stock, you can use seasoning cubes mixed in water instead. Seasoning cubes are available as small packets. These are very salty, so taste the dish after adding the cube before you put more salt. Always crush the seasoning cube to a powder before using it.

**Black Bean Sauce:** This sauce is made from fermented black bean and has a pungent and salty flavour. The black bean is a proprietary product and cannot be made at home. It is available ready made in bottles, at most leading supermarkets.

**Hoisin Sauce:** Hoisin sauce is a thick, reddish-brown, sweet and spicy sauce. It is widely used in Chinese cooking. It's a mixture of soyabeans, plums, garlic, peppers and various spices and is easily available at leading provision stores. In absence of it you can use tomato ketchup, but the taste won"t be that good as with hoisin sauce.

# STARTERS & DIPS

## An accompaniment to Chinese starters...

## Sweet Chilli Dip

*A thin dipping sauce for starters.*

**3 tbsp sugar, ¼ cup water**
**1 tbsp honey**
**1 tsp soya sauce**
**4 tbsp white vinegar**
**1-2 tbsp oil**
**6-8 flakes garlic - crushed to a paste (1 tsp)**
**½ tsp chilli powder, ¼ tsp salt**
**1-2 fresh or dry red chillies - very finely chopped or shredded**

1. Boil sugar and water till sugar dissolves.
2. Add honey and simmer for 1 minute.
3. Add all other ingredients and remove from fire. Serve.

# Green Dim Sums

*A steamed Chinese snack. Use a steamer basket or an idli stand for steaming them.*

*Makes 14 pieces*

**DOUGH**
**1 cup maida, 1 tbsp oil**
**1 cup copped spinach (paalak)**
**½ tsp salt, ¼ tsp sugar, ¼ cup water**

**FILLING**
**2 tbsp oil, 1 onion - finely chopped**
**½ cup finely chopped cauliflower**
**1 large carrot - very finely chopped or grated**
**2 green chillies - finely chopped, 1 tsp ginger-garlic paste**
**2 cups very finely chopped cabbage (½ small cabbage)**
**1 tsp salt & ½ tsp pepper powder, or to taste, 1 tsp vinegar, or to taste**

**DIP SAUCE**
**4-5 tbsp soya sauce, 2 tbsp white vinegar**
**1 tbsp oil, preferably sesame oil**
**4 flakes garlic - crushed to a paste**
**2 tsp tomato ketchup, ½ tsp chilli pd, ¼ tsp salt**

1. For dough, cook spinach with salt, sugar and water for 2-3 minutes till soft. Remove from fire. Let it cool down. Grind to a puree. Sift maida with salt. Add oil. Mix. Add spinach puree *very gradually*, adding just enough that is required to form a dough. Knead well to a stiff dough of rolling consistency, as that for puris.

2. For the filling, heat oil. Add chopped onion. Stir fry till soft. Add cauliflower and cook further for 2 minutes. Add carrot, green chillies & ginger-garlic paste. Mix well and add the cabbage. Stir fry on high flame for 3 minutes. Add salt, pepper to taste. Add vinegar and mix well. Remove from fire and keep filling aside.

3. Take out the dough and form small balls. Roll out flat, as thin as possible into small rounds of 3" diameter.

4. Put some stuffing on a side. Fold the other side to get a semi circle. Put pleats or folds on one open side of the semi circle and press with the other side to seal the snack to get a *gujiya* shape. Turn the pointed edges or corners a little to get rounded edges.

**Final Recipe**

5. To steam, put them in idli stands or a steamer basket and steam for 10 minutes.

6. To prepare dip sauce, mix all ingredients in a bowl. Serve dimsums with dip.

# *Crispy Cinnamon Cauliflower*

### Serves 4

**1 small cauliflower - cut into medium florets with long, thin stems (flat pieces)**

### BATTER
**6 tbsp cornflour**
**4 tbsp plain flour (maida), 4 tbsp suji (semolina)**
**2-3" stick cinnamon (dalchini) - powdered (1 tsp)**
**1 tsp garlic - crushed, 1 tsp salt, ½ tsp pepper, ¼ tsp ajinomoto, optional**
**½ cup water, approx.**

### RED CHILLI-GARLIC PASTE
**3-4 flakes garlic**
**2 dry red chillies - broken into pieces and deseeded**
**1" stick cinnamon (dalchini) - broken into pieces**

### OTHER INGREDIENTS
**2 spring onions - chop white and cut greens separately into ¼" pieces diagonally**
**1 tbsp soya sauce, 1 tbsp tomato sauce, ½ tbsp vinegar**
**½ tsp salt, ¼ tsp ajinomoto**

1. Cut cauliflower into medium flat florets. Wash and wipe dry on a clean towel.
2. Make a thick coating batter in a big bowl by mixing all ingredients of batter with a little water.
3. Heat oil in a kadhai for deep frying.
4. Mix cauliflower in the prepared batter nicely. Deep fry half of the cauliflower at a time, on medium flame till golden and cooked. Remove on paper napkins and keep aside.

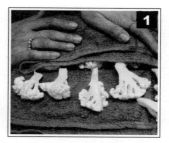

5. For the red chilli - garlic paste, soak all ingredients together in ¼ cup water for 10 minutes and grind to a paste along with the water.
6. Crush dalchini to a powder.
7. Heat 2 tbsp oil in the pan. Add white of spring onions. Stir for a minute till soft.
8. Add red chilli- garlic paste. Stir for ½ minute.
9. Reduce heat. Add soya sauce, tomato sauce and vinegar. Add salt and ajinomoto.
10. Add greens of onions. Mix well.
11. Add ¼ cup water. Stir. Add fried cauliflower and mix well. Serve hot.

# Spring Rolls

*Picture on page 22*      *Serves 4*

**PANCAKES**
½ cup plain flour (maida), ¼ tsp salt
1 cup milk
a pinch of soda-bi-carb (mitha soda)
oil for shallow frying

**VEGETABLE FILLING**
1 onion - chopped finely
8 french beans - shred diagonally
½ cup moong bean sprouts
½ carrot - shredded (cut into very thin long pieces)
½ cup shredded cabbage
½ cup shredded capsicum
a pinch of ajinomoto (optional)
½ tsp white pepper
salt to taste
½ tsp sugar
1 tsp soya sauce
2 tbsp oil

1.  To prepare the pancakes, sift plain flour and salt. Add milk gradually, beating well to make a smooth thin batter. Add soda-bi-carb. Mix well.
2.  Heat a small nonstick pan, taking care not to heat it too much. Smear 1 tsp oil on it all over at the bottom.
3.  Remove the pan from fire and put 1 karchhi batter on it to get a 5" diameter round. Tilt the pan to spread the batter evenly. Return to heat.
4.  Remove the pancake from the pan when the underside is cooked. Do not cook the other side. Make all the other pancake in the same way. Cool. Keep pancakes on a dry cloth or greased aluminium foil, keeping the cooked side on top.
5.  For filling, heat oil. Add onion, cook till soft. Add beans, cook for a minute.
6.  Add sprouts and stir fry for 1 minute. Add ajinomoto, pepper, salt, sugar, carrot, cabbage and capsicum. Stir fry for 1 minute. Add soya sauce. Mix.
7.  To assemble the spring roll, spread a pancake on a flat surface with the cooked side on top. Spread some filling thinly.
8.  Fold in ½" from the right and left sides.
9.  Holding on, fold the top part to cover the filling. Roll on to get a rectangular parcel; making sure that all the filling is enclosed.

10. Seal edges with cornflour paste, made by dissolving 1 tsp of cornflour in 1 tsp of water. If you chill for ½ hour, it keeps better shape.
11. Repeat for the remaining pancakes and filling. Cover all with a plastic wrap/ cling film and keep aside till serving time.
12. Heat some oil in a large frying pan. Reduce heat and put the rolls, folded side down first in oil. Cook on both sides until crisp and golden. Drain on absorbent paper. Serve with red sesame dip given below.

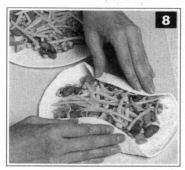 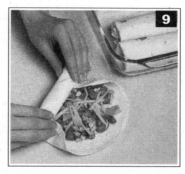

# Red Sesame Dip

**1 tsp saboot dhania - crushed**
**2-3 flakes garlic - chopped**
**2 tsp sesame seeds (til)**
**2 dry red chillies - broken into small pieces and deseeded**
**4 tbsp ready made tomato puree**
**2 tbsp oil**

**ADD LATER**
**¼ tsp salt**
**½ tsp sugar**
**1½ tbsp vinegar**
**½ tsp soya sauce**
**1 tsp sesame oil (optional)**

1. Heat oil. Add crushed saboot dhania and sesame seeds. Stir till seeds turn golden.
2. Reduce heat, add garlic and red chillies. Stir till red chillies turn blackish and garlic changes colour.
3. Add tomato puree. Cook for 3-4 minutes or till dry and oil separates. Remove from fire. Let it cool. Put chilli-tomato mixture in a mixer.
4. Add salt, sugar, vinegar, soya sauce and 2 tbsp water to the mixer. Grind all together to a paste. Check salt.
5. Remove to a bowl. Add 1 tsp sesame oil and mix, if using.

# Chinese Potato Rolls

*Serves 8*

**ROLLS**
4 medium potatoes - boiled & mashed well
3 tbsp cornflour
1 green chilli - deseeded & chopped
2 tbsp coriander - chopped
3/4 tsp salt
½ tsp pepper

**SAUCE**
1 tbsp oil
6-8 flakes garlic - crushed
1 green chilli - deseeded & chopped
2 tbsp tomato ketchup, 1 tsp red chilli sauce
1½ tbsp soya sauce
¼ tsp salt, ¼ tsp pepper
1 tsp cornflour dissolved in ½ cup water
2 tbsp coriander - chopped

1. Mash and mix potatoes with all the ingredients for the rolls.
2. With wet hands, shape into small rolls, of about 1" size. Make the sides slightly flat.
3. Deep fry in medium hot oil to golden brown. Keep aside.
4. For the sauce, heat 1 tbsp oil in a pan. Reduce flame. Add garlic and green chillies.
5. When garlic changes colour, remove from fire.
6. Add tomato ketchup, chilli sauce and soya sauce. Return to fire and add salt, pepper. Cook the sauces for ½ minute.

7. Add cornflour dissolved in water. Add chopped coriander.
8. Simmer for a minute till thick.
9. Add the fried rolls and stir till the sauce coats the rolls, for about 1 minute. Serve

**Note:** Advance work can be done upto step 7, but thicken the sauce and add the rolls to the sauce at the time of serving. If the rolls are in the sauce for too long, they turn limp.

# Leafy Wraps

*A cold snack. A treat on a hot summer day.*

*Serves 6*

**½ cup short grained rice ( or ordinary permal rice)**
**a bunch of lettuce leaves - dipped in cold water & refrigerated for 3 hours till crisp**

**SEASONING FOR RICE**
**1½ tsp white vinegar, 1 tbsp sugar, ½ tsp salt**

**FILLING**
**1 cup finely chopped mushrooms or paneer**
**1 tsp finely chopped garlic**
**1 big onion - chopped finely**
**salt & pepper to taste**
**¼ tsp soya sauce, ½ tsp vinegar**

1.  Wash rice several times in water. Drain. Keep in a strainer for ½ hour.
2.  Put in a pan with 2¼ cups water. Boil. Cover and cook on low heat for about 10 minutes, till water gets absorbed and the rice is soft.
3.  Mix all the seasoning ingredients together. Heat slightly. Do not boil. Remove from fire. Stir till the sugar gets completely dissolved. Let it cool down.
4.  Spread rice in a tray. Pour the cooled dressing over the rice and mix with a fork gently but thoroughly. Let it sit for 15-20 min.
5.  For filling, heat 3 tbsp oil. Add garlic, onion and mushrooms/paneer. Stir for 2-3 minutes. Add salt, pepper, soya sauce and vinegar to taste.

6.  Take a 3" rectangular piece of lettuce leaf (trim the stalk side of the leaf to get a rectangular shape). Place the wrong side up on a flat surface.
7.  Smear or rub some oil on the leaf.
8.  Place 2 tbsp rice on the leaf, leaving the edges. Put a row of vegetable filling on the rice, about 1" wide in the centre. Do not cover the rice completely with the filling. Let all four sides of the rice show.

9.  Roll the leaf starting from the stalk end, moving towards the top to get a roll. Keep aside with the joint side down. Insert a toothpick in the centre to secure the wrap/roll.
10. Serve wraps/rolls cold or at room temperature with sweet chilli dip given on page 13.

# Crunchy Bread Balls

*Picture on facing page*                    *Makes 10 pieces*

**1 tbsp chopped onion, 1 tsp grated ginger**
**1 small green chilli - finely chopped**
**1 small kheera - peeled, cut into 4 lengthwise, deseeded and chopped very finely**
**4 tbsp roasted peanuts (moongphali) - crushed**
**1 potato - boiled and mashed (½ cup)**
**½ tsp soya sauce**
**1 tbsp Chinese 5 spice powder (given below)**
**½ tsp salt or to taste**
**2 tbsp oil**

**OTHER INGREDIENTS**
**5 white bread slices, oil for deep frying**

**5 SPICE POWDER - ROAST TOGETHER AND GRIND TO A COARSE POWDER**
**1 tsp peppercorns (saboot kali mirch)**
**4 star anise (phool chakri), 3 cloves (laung)**
**3" stick cinnamon (dalchini), 1 tsp fennel (saunf)**

1. Heat 2 tbsp oil in a frying pan, add the onion and ginger. Stir fry for 1 minute.
2. Add the green chilli, kheera and peanuts and stir fry for 2 minutes.
3. Add the mashed potatoes, soya sauce, 5 spice powder and salt. Mix well.
4. Cool, divide into 8 equal balls and keep aside.
5. Remove sides of each bread slice and cut into 2 from the middle.
6. Place one piece of bread in the palm of your hand, put a ball of the potato mixture, press the bread around the ball to cover it completely.
7. Repeat with the remaining balls. Deep fry in hot oil till they turn golden brown. Drain on absorbent paper. Serve hot.

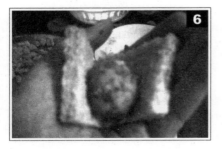
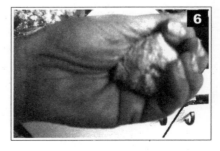

*Glass Noodles with Sesame Paste: Recipe on page 115* ➢
*Crunchy Bread Balls* ➢

# Lotus Wings

*Serves 4*

**200 gm lotus stem (bhein) - peeled & cut diagonally into thin slices**
**2 spring onions - cut white part into rings and greens into 1" diagonal pieces, (keep greens separate)**
**1-2 green chillies - chopped finely**
**4-5 flakes garlic - crushed (optional)**
**¼ tsp each of ajinomoto, salt, pepper, sugar**
**1 tbsp soya sauce, 1 tbsp red chilli sauce**
**1½ tbsp tomato ketchup, ½ tbsp vinegar**
**1 tbsp honey**
**1 tbsp coriander - chopped**

**BATTER**
**4 tbsp plain flour (maida), 4 tbsp cornflour**
**2 flakes garlic - crushed to a paste**
**½ tsp salt, ¼ tsp pepper**

1. Cut lotus stem diagonally into thin slices.
2. To parboil lotus stem, boil 4 cups water with 1 tsp salt. Add sliced lotus stem to boiling water. Boil for 2 minutes. Strain. Refresh in cold water. Strain and keep aside. Wipe dry on a clean kitchen towel.
3. Cut white bulb of spring onion into rings and cut green part diagonally into 1" pieces.

4. For batter- mix maida, cornflour, garlic, salt & pepper. Add just enough water, to make a batter of a thick coating consistency, such that it coats the slices.
5. Dip each piece in batter. Deep fry in two batches to a golden yellow colour. Keep aside.
6. Heat 2 tbsp oil in pan. Reduce heat. Fry the green chillies and garlic till garlic just starts to change colour. Add white of spring onions. Add ajinomoto, salt, pepper and sugar.

7. Remove from fire. Add soya sauce, red chilli sauce, tomato ketchup and vinegar. Return to fire. Stir for a few seconds.
8. Add greens of spring onion. Stir for few seconds.
9. Add honey and mix.
10. Add fried lotus stem and coriander. Mix well till dry and the sauce coats the lotus stem. Remove from heat. Serve hot.

◁ *Spring Rolls : Recipe on page 16*

# *Fried Rice Triangles*

Picture on page 52                    Serves 6-8

### 6 PANCAKES
¾ cup maida, 1¼ cups milk
a pinch of baking powder, ½ tsp salt, ¼ tsp pepper

### FILLING
½ cup uncooked rice - boiled and cooled, deep fried till crisp golden
4 tsp butter, 2 onions - finely chopped
2 tsp ginger-garlic paste
2 tsp soya sauce, 2 tsp vinegar, ¼ tsp ajinomoto
¾ cup coriander - finely chopped, 2-3 spring onion greens only - finely chopped
1 tsp salt and ½ tsp pepper

### TO ASSEMBLE
2 tsp red chilli sauce
¼ cup maida dissolved in ½ cup water, 4-5 tbsp oil to fry

1. For the pancakes, mix all ingredients till well blended. Keep aside for 10 minutes. Heat a non stick pan with 1 tsp oil. Remove from fire and pour 1 karchhi full of batter. Rotate the pan gently to spread the batter to a slightly thick pancake of about 5" diameter. Return to fire and cook the pancake till the edges turn light brown. Remove the pancake from the pan, cooking it only on one side. Make 4 such pancakes. Keep on a greased aluminium foil.
2. Boil rice. Let it cool down. Deep fry in medium hot oil till crisp golden. Drain on a paper napkin. Keep aside.
3. Heat butter. Add onions, stir for 2 minutes. Add ginger-garlic paste, soya sauce, vinegar and ajinomoto.
4. Add coriander, greens of spring onions and deep fried rice. Mix well. Add salt and pepper to taste. Remove from fire.
5. Place the pancake on a flat surface, with the brown side up.
6. Spread chilli sauce on half of the pancake. Leave the other side of the pancake without any sauce.
7. Spread 2-3 tbsp of the rice mixture on the chilli sauce side.
8. Pick up the side without the filling and fold to get a semi circle. Press well so that the edges stick together. Keep aside.
9. Mix ¼ cup maida with ½ cup water in a flat plate.
10. At serving time, heat 4 tbsp oil in a pan. Dip pancake in maida batter on both sides. Shallow fry one pancake at a time carefully till crisp golden on both sides.
11. Cut each fried pancake semicircle into 3 triangular pieces, sprinkle some grated cheese and dot with sauce. Serve hot.

# *Crispy Vegetables*

*Strips of vegetables, thinly batter fried to get crisp fritters with the colourful vegetable showing nicely. Serve with a thin dipping sauce, but do not soak the crisp vegetable for too long in the sauce that it starts to weep!*

*Serves 4*

**4 thick baby corns - cut into 2 lengthwise or 8 thin pieces (do not cut)**
**1 large capsicum - cut into 8 pieces or squares**
**¼ of a small cauliflower - cut into flat pieces**
**1 carrot - cut lengthwise into 2" long flat slices**
**2-3 cabbage leaves - each leaf torn into 2-3 pieces**
**4 spinach leaves with a little stalk**
**1 small brinjal (baingan) - cut into thin flat slices**

**THIN COATING BATTER**
**½ cup cornflour**
**2 tbsp plain flour**
**1 tsp ginger-garlic paste**
**½ tsp salt, ¼ tsp white pepper powder**
**1 tsp soya sauce, ½ tsp vinegar**
**1 tsp lemon juice**
**ice cold water to make the batter**

**DIPPING SAUCE**
**¼ cup vinegar, ¼ cup water**
**1 tsp oil, 2 tsp soya sauce**
**2 tsp tomato ketchup**
**½ tsp garlic paste**
**1 fresh or dry red chilli - minced or very finely chopped**
**1 tsp salt, 1 tsp sugar**

1.  Mix all ingredients of the batter, adding enough ice cold water (about ¼ to ½ cup) to get a batter of pouring consistency. Do not make the batter to thick or too thin.
2.  Dip the vegetable strips in batter and mix well. The batter should coat the vegetables lightly. If not, sprinkle 2 tbsp more cornflour on the vegetables and mix well.
3.  Deep fry 5-6 pieces in hot oil till pale golden (whitish). See that the vegetables are covered very thinly with batter and show even after frying. Do not make them dark brown. Remove on paper napkin and serve with dipping sauce.
4.  To prepare the dip sauce, mix all ingredients in a bowl. Serve vegetables with dipping sauce.

# Salt & Pepper Vegetable

## Serves 4

**1 packet babycorns (100 gm) and 1 packet mushrooms (100 gms) OR 200 gms of any one vegetable**
**¾ cup dry breadcrumbs mixed with ½ tsp salt and ¼ tsp pepper**

### BATTER
6 tbsp cornflour, 1½ tbsp plain flour (maida)
4-5 whole saboot kali mirch (peppercorns) - crushed
1½ tbsp tomato ketchup
¾ tsp soya sauce, ¾ tsp garlic or ginger paste
¾ tsp salt, a pinch of ajinomoto, optional
½-¼ cup water, approx.

### OTHER INGREDIENTS
2-3 tbsp butter
1 onion - cut into 4 pieces
½ tsp salt, ½ tsp freshly crushed peppercorns (saboot kali mirch)
a pinch of ajinomoto
a drop of soya sauce, ½ tsp tomato sauce, 1 tsp vinegar
1 small capsicum - chopped finely

1. Cut a thin slice from the head end (not the pointed end) from each baby corn. Trim the stalk end of each mushroom. Keep vegetables whole. Wash and wipe well on a clean kitchen towel.
2. Make a thick coating batter by mixing all ingredients of batter with a little water.
3. Spread ½ of the breadcrumb mixture in a plate.
4. Dip half the babycorns or mushrooms in the prepared batter and then roll over dry bread crumbs. When breadcrumbs get finished spread the remaining bread crumbs also and repeat for the remaining babycorns or mushrooms.

5. Heat 3 tbsp oil in a pan. Remove pan from fire & swirl or rotate the pan so as to coat bottom of pan nicely with oil. Return to fire.

6. Shallow fry 5- 6 pieces of babycorns or mushrooms at a time in a pan on medium flame till golden and cooked. Remove on paper napkins using a pair of tongs. Keep aside.
7. Heat butter in a pan. Add onion and cook till soft.
8. Reduce heat. Add salt, pepper, ajinomoto, soya sauce, tomato sauce, vinegar and 1 tbsp water. Mix well.

9. Add mushrooms, babycorns and chopped capsicum. Sprinkle ¼ tsp pepper, mix well and serve hot.

# Sesame Gold Coins

**Servings 12**  **Picture on page 42**

**6 bread slices**
**1 tbsp butter or enough to spread**
**1 small onion - chopped finely**
**1 carrot - chopped finely (diced)**
**2 small potatoes - boiled and grated**
**½ tsp soya sauce, 1 tsp vinegar**
**½ tsp pepper, ¼ tsp chilli powder, salt to taste**
**1 capsicum - chopped finely (diced)**
**sesame seeds (til) - to sprinkle**
**chilli garlic tomato sauce to dot**

1. Heat 1½ tbsp oil. Add onions. Cook till transparent.
2. Add carrot and cook for 2- 3 minutes on low flame.
3. Add potatoes, soya sauce, vinegar, salt, pepper, chilli powder and capsicum. Cook for 2-3 minutes. Keep aside.
4. With a cutter or a sharp lid, cut out small rounds (about 1½" diameter) of the bread. Butter both sides of each piece lightly.
5. Spread some potato mixture on the round piece of bread. Press. Sprinkle sesame seeds. Press. Grill for about 7-8 minutes till bread turns golden on the edges and crisp from the under side. Serve, dotted with chilli-garlic sauce.

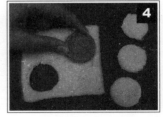

**Final Recipe**

# Corn Rolls

*Cream Style Corn is filled in flattened bread slices and pan fried. This starter is made using cream style corn which is otherwise used commonly for making sweet corn soup. In cream style corn, most of the corn kernels are crushed. It is different from tinned corn which has whole corn kernels.*

*Picture on page 129*　　　　　　　　*Makes 8 pieces*

**4 pieces of fresh bread**

**FILLING**
**1 tin cream style sweet corn, use 1 cup, see note**
**1 onion - finely chopped**
**½ tsp garlic paste**
**1 green chilli - deseeded & finely chopped**
**½ tsp soya sauce**
**½ tsp salt, ¼ tsp pepper to taste**
**½ tsp vinegar**
**2 tbsp oil**

1. Heat oil in a pan, add onion. Cook till onion turns golden.
2. Add garlic paste and green chilli, cook for 1 minute on medium flame.
3. Add 1 cup cream style sweet corn. Mix well.
4. Add soya sauce, salt and pepper and vinegar. Mix well and cook for 2 minutes on medium flame. Cool.
5. Cut the sides of a slice, keep it flat on a rolling board.
6. Press, applying pressure with a rolling pin (belan) so that the holes of the bread close. Keep aside. Similarly roll the other slices.
7. Spread a layer of the filling on each bread. Press the filling. Roll carefully.
8. Cut edges of the roll to neaten them.
9. Pan fry/ deep fry each roll in hot oil till golden.
10. Now cut each roll into 2 pieces and serve hot.

**Note:** The leftover corn, can be stored in an air tight box in the freezer compartment of the fridge for about 2 months or till further use.

# Steps of Corn Rolls

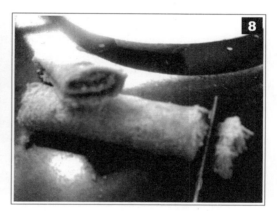

# *Momos*

*Picture on facing page*                    Makes 12

**DOUGH**
**1 cup maida (plain flour), 1 tbsp oil, ¼ tsp salt**

**FILLING**
**2 tbsp oil**
**1 onion - finely chopped**
**6 mushrooms - chopped finely**
**1 large carrot - very finely chopped or grated**
**2 green chillies - finely chopped**
**1 tsp ginger-garlic paste**
**2 cups very finely chopped cabbage (½ small cabbage)**
**1 tsp salt & ½ tsp pepper powder, or to taste**

1.  Sift maida with salt. Add oil and knead with enough water to make a stiff dough of rolling consistency, as that for puris.
2.  For the filling, heat oil in the kadhai. Add the chopped onion. Fry till it turns soft. Add mushrooms and cook further for 2 minutes. Add carrot, green chillies and ginger-garlic paste. Mix well and add the cabbage. Stir fry on high flame for 3 minutes. Add salt, pepper to taste. Remove from fire and keep the filling aside.
3.  Make marble sized balls and roll as thin as possible, to make about 5 inch rounds. Put 1 heaped tbsp of the filling. Pick up the sides into loose folds like frills and keep collecting each fold in the centre, to give a flattened ball (like kachorie) shape. Make all momos and keep aside.
4.  Place the momos in a greased idli stand or a steamer basket. Fill a large pan with a little water, about 1" at the bottom and place the momos in it. Cover the pan and boil water (steam) on medium flame for about 8-10 minutes.
5.  Check with a knife. If the knife is clean, remove from fire.
6.  Momos can be had steamed, or can be baked in the oven at 200°C for 5 minutes till light golden on the edges. Serve with chutney given below.

**RED HOT CHUTNEY**
**2-3 dry, Kashmiri red chillies - soaked in ¼ cup warm water**
**6-8 flakes garlic**
**1 tsp saboot dhania (coriander seeds)**
**1 tsp jeera (cumin seeds),**
**1 tbsp oil, ½ tsp salt, 1 tsp sugar**
**½ tsp soya sauce, 3 tbsp vinegar**

For the chutney, grind the soaked red chillies along with the water, garlic, dhania, jeera, oil, salt and sugar to a paste. Add soya sauce and vinegar to taste.

# *Spicy Skewers*

*Serves 12*          *Picture on opposite page*

**150 gms paneer - cut into 1" squares**
**100 gm baby corns - cut into 2 pieces widthwise**
**1 large capsicum - cut into ½" pieces**
**1 tomato - pulp removed and cut into ½" pieces**
**3 tbsp oil**
**4-5 flakes garlic - crushed**
**1 tbsp vinegar, 1½ tbsp soya sauce**
**3 tbsp tomato ketchup**
**½ tbsp chilli sauce**
**½ tsp salt and ½ tsp pepper, or to taste**

**THICK COATING BATTER**
**¼ cup maida**
**½ tsp salt, ¼ pepper, ¼ cup water**

1. Cut paneer into 1" squares, capsicum cut into ½" pieces.
2. Cut baby corns widthwise into half to get 2 pieces.
3. Mix all ingredients of the coating batter.

4. Dip the paneer and babycorns in maida batter and deep fry till golden brown. Keep aside.
5. Heat 3 tbsp oil. Reduce heat. Add garlic. Let it turn light brown.

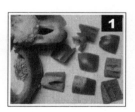

6. Remove from fire. Add vinegar, soya sauce, tomato ketchup, chilli sauce, salt and pepper. Return to fire and cook the sauces on low heat for ½ minute.
7. Add baby corns. Stir for 2-3 minutes.
8. Add capsicum, paneer and tomato pieces. Mix well. Stir for 1-2 minutes. Remove from fire.

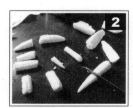

9. Thread (pass) a capsicum, then a baby corn, then a paneer and lastly a tomato piece on each tooth pick. Serve.

# *Honey Rice Balls*

*Picture on page 2*        *Makes 14*

**1 cups uncooked rice of short grained quality (permal rice)**
**2 flakes garlic - crushed (optional)**
**2 green chillies - chopped finely**
**¼ cup very finely sliced french beans**
**1 carrot - finely diced (cut into tiny pieces)**
**½ big capsicum - diced (cut into tiny pieces)**
**1½ tsp of salt, ¼ tsp pepper**
**¼ tsp ajinomoto (optional)**
**2 tbsp soya sauce**
**3 tbsp honey**
**1 tbsp vinegar, 1½ tsp chilli sauce**
**1½ tbsp cornflour**

**COATING**
**4 tbsp maida mixed with ½ cup water**
**1 tsp soya sauce, ¼ tsp salt, a pinch pepper**
**½ cup sesame seeds (til)**

1. Boil 8-10 cups water with 2 tsp salt. Wash and add rice and cook till very soft. Drain rice and keep aside in the strainer.
2. Heat 2 tbsp oil. Reduce heat. Stir fry garlic and green chillies for ½ minute.
3. Add beans and carrots. Stir fry for 1 minute. Add capsicum. Mix.
4. Add salt, pepper and ajinomoto. Mix well.
5. Add rice. Sprinkle soya sauce on the rice and mix well mashing it in between.
6. Pour honey, vinegar and chilli sauce on the rice and mix well.
7. Sprinkle cornflour and mix well. Remove from fire and let the rice cool down. After it cools down, mash rice well with hands so that it starts to bind and can be formed into a ball.
8. Make marble sized balls with wet hands.
9. Make a thin maida batter by mixing maida with water in a bowl. Add soya sauce, salt and pepper to the batter.
10. Scatter 2 tbsp sesame seeds on a plate. Do not spread all the seeds at one time.
11. Dip the balls in maida batter and immediately roll over the scattered sesame seeds. Roll the ball on the seasme seeds using only the fingers so as to stick the seeds nicely allover the ball. Keep aside till serving time.
12. Deep fry 1-2 balls at a time on medium flame till golden brown and crisp. Remove on paper napkins and serve with red chilli sauce.

# Steps of Honey Rice Balls

# SOUPS

## Garnish for Soups

### FRIED NOODLES
½ cup raw noodles can be deep fried on medium heat till golden. Top a cup or a bowl of soup with 1-2 tbsp of these fried noodles to add crunch to the soup

### FINELY CHOPPED SPRING ONION GREENS
Chop a green stalk of spring onion very finely and top soup with 1 tsp of these.

### GOLDEN TOFU CUBES
Cut tofu or paneer into tiny cubes of ¼" and deep fry till golden.

## Helpful Hints

If the soup appears thin, dissolve 1-2 tsp cornflour in a little tap water and add to the boiling soup. Stir on low medium heat till the soup thickens.

Vegetables in soup taste good if they are crunchy or cooked till just crisp-tender. Never boil the soup too much after adding the vegetables as the vegetables turn soft on doing so.

A seasoning cube added to the soup makes a lot of difference in the taste. Keep stock cubes handy in the fridge.

# Fresh Vegetable Stock

*Makes 6 cups*

**1 onion - chopped**
**1 carrot - chopped, 1 potato - chopped**
**4-5 french beans - chopped**
**or**
**½ cup chopped cabbage**
**½ tsp crushed garlic - optional**
**1 tsp crushed ginger, ½ tsp salt**
**7 cups water**

1. Mix all ingredients & pressure cook for 10-15 minutes.
2. Do not mash the vegetables if a clear soup is to be prepared. Strain and use as required.

# Quick Veg Stock

*Soup cubes or seasoning cubes may be boiled with water and used instead of the stock, if you are short of time. These seasoning cubes are easily available in the market and are equally good in taste.*

*Makes 2½ cups*

**1 vegetable seasoning cube (maggi, knorr or any other, SEE NOTE)**
**2½ cups of water**

1. Crush 1 vegetable seasoning cube roughly in a pan.
2. Add 2½ cups of water and give one boil. Use as required.

**Note:** The seasoning cube has a lot of salt, so reduce salt if you substitute this stock with the fresh stock. Check taste before adding salt.

# Vegetable Sweet Corn Soup
## ( with Tinned Corn )
### Serves 6-8

**1 tin (450 gm) sweet corn - cream style**
**1½ tbsp vinegar**
**½ tsp ajinomoto (optional)**
**½ tsp sugar - optional**
**2½ tsp salt, or to taste**
**½ tsp white pepper**
**5 cups water**
**4 level tbsp cornflour dissolved in 1 cup of water**

1. Open the corn tin. Churn just for a **second** in a grinder, so that most of the corn kernels are roughly crushed, and a few corns are left whole too.
2. Mix corn and water in a pan. Boil for 3-4 minutes.
3. Add vinegar, ajinomoto, sugar, salt and pepper.
4. Mix cornflour in water and add to the soup, stirring continuously.
5. Cook for 8-10 minutes, stirring occasionally.
6. More cornflour may be dissolved in a little water and added to the boiling soup, if the soup appears thin. Boil for 3-4 minutes after adding the cornflour paste.
7. Serve hot with green chillies in vinegar.

# Green Chillies in Vinegar

### Makes ½ cup

**¼ cup white vinegar**
**½ tsp salt**
**½ tsp sugar**
**2-3 drops soya sauce**
**2-3 green chillies**

1. Chop green chillies finely.
2. Mix all other ingredients.
3. Add green chillies.
4. Heat on fire till it is about to boil.
5. Remove from fire. Serve in a small bowl.

# Kimchi Salad

*Serves 4*

**½ of a medium cabbage - cut into 1½" square pieces**
**2 tsp salt, 2 tsp sugar**
**2 tsp Soya sauce**
**1 tsp vinegar**
**2 tbsp tomato ketchup**
**½ tsp salt and ¼ tsp pepper, or to taste**
**¼ tsp ajinomotto**

**GRIND TOGETHER TO A PASTE**
**2 dry red chillies - deseeded and soaked in water for 10 minutes**
**1 tsp chopped ginger**
**1 tsp chopped garlic**

1.  Boil 4-5 cups of water with 2 tsp salt and 2 tsp sugar. Add cabbage to boiling water. Remove from fire. Strain and refresh the cabbage in cold water. Leave it in the strainer for 15 minutes for the water to drain out completely.
2.  Drain the red chillies. Grind red chillies with ginger and garlic to a smooth paste using a little water.
3.  To the red chilli paste, add Soya sauce, vinegar, tomato ketchup, salt, pepper and ajinomoto.
4.  Add the paste to the cabbage and toss lightly so that the paste coats the cabbage. Serve at room temperature.

# Hot & Sour Vegetable Soup

*The popular Chinese soup. An all time favourite!*

*Picture on facing page*                    *Serves 6*

**TOMATO STOCK**
**2 big tomatoes - chopped, 6 cups water**

**CHILLI-GARLIC PASTE**
**2 dry red chillies - deseeded and soaked in water for 10 minutes**
**2 flakes garlic, 1 tsp vinegar**

**OTHER INGREDIENTS**
**1 tomato - chopped very finely**
**1 tbsp finely sliced french beans**
**½ cup chopped cabbage**
**½ cup grated carrot**
**1-2 tbsp dried mushrooms - optional**
**½ tsp ajinomoto (optional)**
**½ tsp sugar**
**1¼ tsp salt and ½ tsp pepper powder, or to taste**
**1½-2 tbsp soya sauce, 1½ tbsp vinegar**
**2 vegetable seasoning cubes (maggi) - powdered**
**4½ tbsp cornflour mixed with ½ cup water**

1. Soak dry, red chillies in little water for 10 minutes.
2. Pressure cook water and tomatoes together to give 2-3 whistles. Strain. Do not mash the tomatoes. Keep the tomato stock aside.
3. For the chilli-garlic paste, drain the red chillies. Grind red chillies, garlic and vinegar to a paste.
4. If dried mushrooms are available, soak them in water for ½ hour to soften.
5. Heat 2 tbsp oil. Add chilli-garlic paste. Stir.
6. Add chopped tomato. Crush while cooking it. Cook for 1 minute.
7. Add beans, soaked mushrooms, cabbage and carrots. Stir fry for 1 minute.
8. Add the prepared tomato stock and the seasoning cubes.
9. Add all the other ingredients except cornflour paste. Boil for 2 minutes.
10. Add cornflour paste, stirring continuously. Cook for 2-3 minutes till the soup turns thick. Serve hot.

# *Vegetable Sweet Corn Soup*

## *(with Fresh Corn)*

*Serves 6*          *Picture on opposite page*

**4 big whole corns-on-the cob (saboot bhutta)**
**½ cup cabbage - shredded**
**½ cup carrots - very finely chopped**
**4 level tbsp cornflour dissolved in 1 cup water**
**2-3 tbsp sugar**
**½ tsp ajinomoto (optional)**
**1-2 tbsp white vinegar**
**½ tsp white pepper**
**salt to taste**

1. Take out a few whole corn kernels and grate the rest of the corn on the grater.
2. Pressure cook grated and whole corn with 6 cups of water and 2 tsp salt.
3. After the first whistle, keep on low heat for 10 minutes. Remove from heat.
4. After the pressure drops, mix cornflour in water and add to cooked corn.
5. Add sugar, ajinomoto, vinegar, white pepper and salt to taste.
6. Give it one boil. Keep it boiling for 5-7 minutes. More cornflour, dissolved in a little water may be added if the soup appears thin.
7. Add the vegetables — cabbage and carrot. Check salt.
8. After adding the vegetables, boil the soup for 2-3 minutes only. Do not overcook the vegetables, leave them crunchy and crisp. Remove from fire.
9. Serve hot with green chillies in vinegar.

### Shredding of Cabbage

**Cut cabbage into 4 pieces. Place a flat side of the ¼ head of cabbage on a cutting board. Cut into thin slices with a large sharp knife. Cut slices several times to make smaller pieces.**

◄ *Sesame Gold Coins : Recipe on page 27*
◄ *Vegetable Sweet Corn Soup*

# Manchow Soup

### Serves 6

**3 tbsp oil**
**4 flakes garlic - crushed (½ tsp)**
**1 tsp very finely chopped ginger**
**1 cup finely chopped mushrooms (6-8 mushrooms)**
**1 cup finely shredded (cut into thin, 1" long pieces) cabbage**
**1½ small carrots - thinly cut into round slices or flowers (1 cup), see page 54**
**salt to taste**
**½ tsp pepper, or to taste**
**a pinch of ajinomoto**
**3-4 drops of soya sauce**
**2 tsp chilli sauce**
**1 tsp vinegar**
**2 vegetable seasoning cubes (maggi, knorr or any other)**
**6 cups water**
**6 tbsp cornflour dissolved in 1 cup water**
**½ cup noodles - deep fried till crisp, for garnish, optional**

1. Heat 3 tbsp oil. Reduce heat. Add garlic and ginger. Stir on low heat.
2. Add mushrooms. Stir for a minute on medium flame. Add cabbage and carrot. Stir for a minute.
3. Reduce heat. Add pepper, ajinomoto, a few drops soya sauce, chilli sauce and vinegar. Stir to mix well.
4. Add 6 cups water and bring to a boil. Crush 2 seasoning cube and add to the boiling water. Mix. Simmer for 2-3 minutes. Check salt and add more according to taste.
5. Add dissolved cornflour. Bring to a boil, stirring constantly. Simmer for 2 minutes.
6. Serve in soup bowls, garnished with some crisp fried noodles.

# *Lemon Coriander Soup*

*Serves 4*

### CLEAR STOCK
5 cups water
1 stick lemon grass - chopped or rind of 1 lemon (1 tsp rind)
¼ cup chopped coriander along with stalks
1" piece of ginger - sliced without peeling
2 laung
1 tej patta
2 seasoning cubes (maggi or knorr or any other brand)

### OTHER INGREDIENTS
1 tsp oil, a pinch of red chilli powder
½ carrot - peeled and cut into paper thin slices diagonally (¼ cup)
2 mushrooms - cut into thin slices, optional (¼ cup)
salt & pepper to taste
2- 3 tbsp lemon juice
¼ tsp sugar
1½ tbsp cornflour dissolved in ¼ cup water
2 tbsp coriander leaves - torn roughly with the hands

1.  If using lemon rind, wash & grate 1 lemon with the peel gently on the grater to get lemon rind. Do not apply pressure and see that the white pith beneath the lemon peel is not grated along with the yellow rind. The white pith is bitter!

2.  For stock, mix all ingredients given under stock with 5 cups of water. Bring to a boil. Keep on low flame for 2-3 minutes. Keep aside.

3.  Heat 1 tsp oil in a pan. Add a pinch of red chilli powder.

4.  Immediately, add carrot and mushrooms cut into paper thin slices. Saute for 1 minute on medium flame.

5.  Add pepper. Check salt and add more if required. Boil.

6.  Strain the prepared stock into the vegetables in the pan.

7.  Add 1½ tbsp cornflour dissolved in ¼ cup water, stirring continuously.

8.  Add lemon juice, sugar and coriander leaves. Simmer for 2 minutes. Add more lemon juice if required. Remove from fire. Serve hot in soup bowls.

# *Wonton Vegetable Soup*

### *Serves 6*

**WONTON WRAPPERS WITHOUT EGGS**
1 cup plain flour *(maida)*
½ tsp salt
1 tbsp oil
a little water (chilled)

**WONTON FILLING**
½ carrot - parboiled & chopped very finely
8 french beans - parboiled & chopped very finely
½ cup cabbage - finely chopped
1 tbsp oil
¼ cup onion - finely chopped
salt to taste
½ tsp white pepper
½ tsp sugar
1 tsp soya sauce
a pinch of ajinomoto (optional)

**WONTON SOUP**
6 cups vegetable stock - recipe on page 36
2 spring onions - chopped
½ cucumber - thinly sliced
1 tbsp soya sauce
1 tsp white pepper
1 tsp sugar
¼ tsp ajinomoto (optional)

1. To prepare the wonton wrappers, sift plain flour and salt.
2. Rub in oil till the flour resembles bread crumbs.
3. Add chilled water gradually and make a stiff dough.
4. Knead the dough well for about 5 minutes till smooth.
5. Cover the dough with a damp cloth and keep aside for ½ hour.
6. To prepare the filling, heat oil. Stir fry onions, for a few seconds.
7. Add all other vegetables. Stir fry for ½ minute.
8. Add salt, pepper, sugar, soya sauce and ajinomoto. Mix and remove from fire.
9. Cool the filling.
10. Divide the dough into 4 balls. Roll out each ball into thin chappatis.
11. Cut into 2" square pieces. Place a little filling in the centre. Fold in half and press

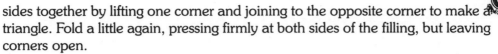

sides together by lifting one corner and joining to the opposite corner to make a triangle. Fold a little again, pressing firmly at both sides of the filling, but leaving corners open.

12. Bring 2 corners together, and cross over infront of the filling. Brush lightly with water where they meet, to make them stick.

13. The wontons may be folded into different shapes like money bags, nurses caps or envelopes. Keep wontons aside.

14. To prepare the soup, boil vegetable stock.

15. Add the prepared wontons. Cover and cook for 12-15 minutes on low flame till they float on the top.

16. Add all the other ingredients. Simmer for 1-2 minutes. Serve hot.

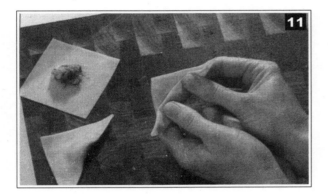

# Stir fried Vegetable Soup

*Serves 4*

**1 cup grated cabbage**
**½ cup grated carrots**
**1 tsp oil**
**1 tsp soya sauce**
**2 tsp chilli sauce**
**½ tsp salt, ½ tsp pepper, or to taste**
**4 cups vegetable stock (see page 37) or water**
**3 tbsp cornflour - dissolved in ½ cup water**
**¼-½ cup paneer - finely diced**
**2 tbsp lemon juice**

1. Grate cabbage and carrot finely.
2. In a pan, heat oil. Add carrot and cabbage. Stir for a minute.
3. Add soya sauce, chilli sauce, salt and pepper. Add 4 cups water. Boil.
4. Dissolve cornflour in ½ cup water, stir well and add the cornflour paste into the soup. Stir till it boils. Remove when the thick.
5. Add some more cornflour dissolved in water, if the soup appears thin.
6. Add tiny cubes of paneer. Add lemon juice and serve hot.

# *Mushroom Ginger Crispy Rice Soup*

*Serves 6*

½ cup boiled rice - spread on a tray for 10 minutes and deep fried till golden
1 cup sliced fresh mushrooms
1 cup bean sprouts
1 tbsp crushed ginger
6 cups vegetable stock (see page 37) or 6 cups of water mixed with 2 vegetable a
seasoning cubes (maggie or knorr)
1 tbsp soya sauce
1 tbsp vinegar
1 tsp sugar
1 tsp white pepper
salt to taste
¼ tsp ajinomoto (optional)
2 tbsp cornflour dissolved in ¼ cup water
2 tbsp oil

1. Prepare vegetable stock as given on page 37.
2. Heat oil. Add mushrooms and bean sprouts. Stir fry for 2 minutes.
3. Add crushed ginger. Stir fry for ½ minute.
4. Add vegetable stock or a seasoning cube (maggi) dissolved in 6 cups of water.
5. Add all the other ingredients except cornflour paste.
6. Boil. Add cornflour paste. Cook for 1 minute till the soup turns thick.
7. Serve soup garnished with fried rice.

# Talomein Soup

*Serves 4*

**4 cups vegetable stock - see page 37**
**½ carrot - parboiled and cut into leaves or cut diagonally into slices - see page 55**
**3-4 cabbage leaves - roughly torn**
**1 cup boiled noodles**
**1 tsp salt, or to taste**
**½ tsp each of sugar, black pepper**
**1 tsp soya sauce**
**a pinch ajinomoto (optional)**
**2 tbsp cornflour dissolved in ½ cup water**

1. Boil 5 cups of water in a large pan. Add 2 tsp salt and 1 tsp sugar to the water. Add peeled carrot to the boiling water. Boil. Keep on boiling for 1-2 minutes. Drain. Refresh in cold water. Cut into thin leaves or diagonal slices. Keep aside.
2. Mix stock, salt, pepper, sugar, soya sauce and ajinomoto in a pan and boil.
3. Add cornflour paste, stirring continuously.
4. Add carrots and cabbage.
5. Boil for 2-3 minutes.
6. Add boiled noodles, remove from fire. Serve.

*Paneer Steak & Mung Beans : Recipe on page 72*  ➤

# VEGETABLE DISHES

## Important Tips...

♦ A Chinese dish will have all the vegetables cut in the same shape, e.g. to prepare any dish with noodles, all the vegetables are always cut into thin long strips. For fried rice, everything is diced — cut into small squares.

♦ Chinese food is crunchy and full of flavour, so never over cook food.

♦ Always use a big pan or wok to stir-fry. This avoids mashing or breaking the food into bits.

♦ Use ajinomoto, the Chinese salt, sparingly. Usually just a pinch is enough. When you double the quantity of the dish, do not double the quantity of ajinomoto.

♦ The amount of soya sauce can be increased or reduced according to the desired colour of the dish. Remember, soya sauce is salty, so keep a check on the salt when you increase the quantity of soya sauce.

◄ *Honey Potato Fingers: Recipe on page 56*
◄ *Fried Rice Triangles: Recipe on page 24*

# Techniques of Cutting Vegetables

The Chinese style of cutting vegetables is based on the principle of exposing maximum surface area so that the food gets cooked quickly, retaining the natural flavour and colour.

## Shredding:

This is one of the typical methods of cutting Chinese food. The vegetables are cut into thin, strips or shreds. Shredded vegetables are commonly seen in **chow mein**. Spinach, lettuce, cabbage are all shredded. Carrot can be grated on the big holes of a grater to get shredded carrot.

## Dicing:

The vegetables are cut into dice or small cubes. The vegetables are first cut lengthwise into ¼ or ½ inch thick strips and several such strips kept together and further cut into ¼ inch pieces. **Fried rice** has diced vegetables.

## Slicing :

The ingredients are cut into thin slices. The thickness depends on what is specified in each individual recipe.

## Diagonal slices:

The vegetables are cut into thin slices in a slanting manner in such a way that there are more exposed surfaces. Vegetables such as a asparagus, carrots, celery of French beans are usually diagonally sliced. Diagonally cut carrots and cucumbers, are commonly seen in **sweet and sour vegetables.**

## Jullienes:

The vegetables are cut into thin slices. The slices are stacked together to get thin match sticks of the vegetables.

## Decorative cutting :

Sometimes carrots and spring onions are cut like flowers and leaves. Red radishes and tomatoes are cut like roses.

a. To make **carrot flowers** take a thick, big carrot and make ¼ inch broad and deep slits at four equidistant places. Carefully, cut the carrot into thin round slices.

b. For **carrot leaves**, cut the carrot lengthwise into thin slices. Cut each slice diagonally into 2-3" pices. Make "V" or notches on the side to get leaves.

c. To make **spring onion flowers**, cut off the green tops and about ¼ inch piece from the other end. Make several slits about ½ inch deep at both ends and place in iced water for some time until the onions open up like flowers.

d. To make **red radish roses**, cut each radish almost all the way into 6-8 petal-like sections. Place in iced water.

# Techniques of Chinese Cooking

### How to parboil vegetables:

Sometimes vegetables are slightly cooked in salted water and then added to the dish. Whole carrots are peeled, beans are threaded and dropped in boiling water for one minute to parboil them. They are then cooled and cut into desired shapes.

### How to use cornflour:

Sometimes, the sauce may appear a little thin. To thicken it, dissolve a little extra cornflour in some water and add it to the boiling sauce. Remember to stir the sauce continuously, when the cornflour paste is being added.

### How to stir-fry food:

Stir frying food, is to cook food on a high flame for a short period, **stirring continuously.** Stir frying of vegetables is done in sequence of their tenderness. e.g. onions are stir fried first, then french beans, then carrots, cabbage and so on. Each vegetable is stir fried for a few seconds, before adding the next vegetable.

# *Honey Potato Fingers*

*A popular dry dish of saucy and crisp golden potato fingers.*

*Picture on page 52*                    Serves 4

**4 large potatoes**

**BATTER**
**¼ cup + 2 tbsp flour (maida), ¼ cup cornflour**
**½ tsp salt, ¼ tsp pepper, a pinch of ajinomoto, ½ tsp soya sauce**
**2 pinches or drops of orange red colour**

**OTHER INGREDIENTS**
**4-5 green chillies - slit lengthwise and deseeded**
**4-5 flakes garlic - crushed, optional**
**1 tsp soya sauce**
**1 tbsp red chilli sauce**
**2½ tbsp tomato ketchup, ½ tbsp vinegar**
**2 tsp honey**
**¼ tsp each of salt and pepper**
**3 greens of spring onions - cut diagonally into 2" pieces**
**1 tbsp chopped coriander**

1. Peel the potatoes and cut into ¼" thick slices. Cut each slice into ¼" wide fingers. Soak them in salted cold water for 15 minutes. Strain and wipe dry on a clean kitchen towel. Sprinkle 1-2 tbsp cornflour on them to absorb excess water.

2. For the batter- mix flour, cornflour, salt, pepper, ajinomoto, soya sauce and colour. Add just enough water, about 3-4 tbsp, to make a batter of a thick pouring consistency, such that it coats the potatoes.

3. Dip fingers of potatoes in the batter and deep fry to a golden orange colour. Check that they get properly cooked on frying. Keep aside, spread out on a plate till the time of serving.

4. At serving time, heat 1 tbsp oil. Reduce heat. Fry the green chillies and garlic till garlic changes colour.

5. Add soya sauce, chilli sauce, tomato ketchup and vinegar. Stir. Add honey.

6. Add salt and pepper. Add 2 tbsp water and greens of spring onions and coriander.

7. Add the fried potatoes. Mix well. Serve hot.

# Vegetable Manchurian

*Vegetable balls in a thin brownish sauce.*

*Serves 6* 　　　*Picture on page 90*

### MANCHURIAN BALLS
**1 cup grated cauliflower**
**¼ cup diced or grated carrots**
**¼ cup finely grated cabbage**
**1-2 slices bread - churned in a mixer to get fresh bread crumbs**
**1 tbsp cornflour**
**1 tbsp flour (maida)**
**¼ tsp ajinomoto, salt and pepper to taste**
**2-3 tbsp milk**

### MANCHURIAN SAUCE
**2 tbsp oil**
**1" piece ginger - crushed to a paste, 5-6 flakes garlic - crushed - optional**
**2 green chillies - chopped**
**½ onion - very finely chopped**
**1 tbsp soya sauce, 1½ tbsp tomato ketchup, 2 tsp vinegar**
**½ tsp salt, ¼ tsp pepper**
**1½ - 2 tbsp cornflour - dissolved in ½ cup water**
**1 spring onion greens - chopped finely, to garnish**

1. Mix all ingredients of the balls, adding only ½ of the churned bread mixture first. (Remaining bread crumbs may be added if balls fall apart on frying.) Add enough milk so that the balls bind together easily. Make oval balls. Flatten each ball.
2. Deep fry 3-4 pieces at a time on medium flame. Reduce flame after the balls turn light brown and fry till cooked and brown. Keep aside.
3. To prepare manchurian sauce, heat 2 tbsp oil. Add ginger and garlic. Fry on low flame for 1 minute.
4. Add green chillies and onions. Cook till they turn light brown.
5. Reduce heat and add soya sauce, tomato ketchup, vinegar, salt and pepper. Cook for 2-3 minutes.
6. Add 1½ cups of water. Boil. Keep on slow fire for 2-3 minutes.
7. Dissolve cornflour in ½ cup water and add to the above sauce, stirring continuously. Cook till slightly thick. Keep the sauce aside.
8. To serve, boil the sauce. Add the balls to the manchurian sauce and keep on slow fire for one minute till the balls are heated through. Serve hot sprinkled with finely chopped spring onion greens with fried rice or noodles.

# Paneer in Five Spice Powder

*A wet dish of crisp fried paneer slices in fragrant spice blend.*

*Serves 4*

**200 gms paneer (whole block weighing 200 gms) - cut into ¼" thick rectangular pieces**

**BATTER**
**3 tbsp cornflour, 2 tbsp plain flour (maida)**
**2 tbsp suji (semolina)**
**½ tsp soya sauce**
**½ tsp crushed garlic**
**½ tsp salt, ¼ tsp ajinomoto, optional**
**¼ cup water, approx.**

**FIVE SPICE POWDER - ROAST TOGETHER AND GRIND TO A COARSE POWDER (MAKES 6 TSP)**
**2 tsp peppercorns (saboot kali mirch)**
**3 star anise (phool chakri)**
**6 laung (cloves)**
**6" stick dalchini (cinnamon), 3 tsp saunf (fennel)**

**OTHER INGREDIENTS**
**4- 5 flakes of garlic - chopped, ½ tsp chopped ginger**
**½ tsp soya sauce, ½ tbsp vinegar**
**¼ tsp ajinomoto, ¾ tsp sugar**
**2 tbsp wine (optional)**
**2 spring onions - chop white and cut greens separately into ¼" pieces diagonally**
**2 cups stock or 2 cups water mixed with 1 seasoning cube**
**2 tbsp cornflour mixed with ½ cup water**

1. For five spice powder, grind all the ingredients of the powder in a small mixer to a powder. Strain the powder through a sieve (channi).
2. Cut the block of paneer into rectangular slices of about ¼" thickness. Do not make the slices too thick.
3. Make a thick coating batter by mixing all ingredients of batter with a little water. From the strained spice powder, put 1¼ tsp in the batter. Mix well.
4. Heat 2 tbsp oil in a pan. Remove pan from fire and swirl or rotate the pan so as to coat the bottom of the pan nicely with oil. Return to fire.
5. Dip paneer in the prepared batter and shallow fry half of the paneer in a pan on medium flame till golden crisp on both sides.
6. Remove on paper napkins. Cut each piece of fried paneer diagonally into two to get 2 triangular pieces. Keep aside.

7. Heat 2 tbsp oil in pan. Add white of spring onions and chopped garlic, ginger, remaining five spice powder. Cook till soft.
8. Shut off the flame, add soya sauce, vinegar, ajinomoto, sugar and wine.
9. Return to fire, add 2 cups stock. Give one boil.
10. Add cornflour paste. Stir for a minute till thick. Add fried paneer and chopped spring onion greens. Mix and serve hot.

# *Baby Corn - Spinach in Caramelized Sauce*

*Serves 4-5*

**1 packet (100 gm) babycorns - keep whole**
**20- 22 leaves of spinach - chop stem and roughly tear each leaf into 2 by hand**
**2-3 dry, red chillies - broken into pieces, deseeded & ground to a rough powder**
**¼ tsp salt**
**5 tbsp chopped walnuts (akhrot)**

**CARAMELIZED SAUCE**
**2 tsp butter, 2 tsp sugar**
**2 medium onions - chopped, 1 tsp chopped garlic**
**a drop of soya sauce, a pinch of ajinomoto, 2 tsp vinegar**
**2 vegetable seasoning cubes (maggi, knorr or any other brand)**
**5 tbsp cornflour**

1. To make stock with cube, boil 4 cups water with 2 vegetable seasoning cubes. Give one boil and remove from fire. Keep aside.
2. Dissolve cornflour in ¼ cup of water and keep aside.
3. Heat 5 tbsp oil in a wok or a kadhai, add dry red chilli powder, stir fry for a minute.
4. Add babycorns and cook covered for 4-5 minutes on medium heat till brown specs appear on the babycorn and they get crisp-tender.
5. Add spinach and stir fry for another 1-2 minutes. Add ¼ salt. Remove from fire.
6. For sauce, heat 2 tsp butter in a pan on low heat, let it get light brown, add 2 tsp sugar, let it melt, wait for a few seconds more till it turns golden.
7. Add chopped onion and chopped garlic. Cook till onion turn soft.
8. Reduce heat, add soya sauce, ajinomoto and vinegar. Mix
9. Add the prepared stock (water mixed with seasoning cube). Bring to a boil.
10. Add cornflour mixed with water. Stir till sauce thickens slightly.
11. Add stir fried babycorn, spinach and chopped walnuts. Mix well, remove from fire. Serve hot.

# *Hoisin Stir Fry Okra*

*Crispy fried okra tossed in a tempting hoisin sauce.*

Serves 4                          Picture on page 4

**250 gms okra (bhindi) - slice into 2 pieces lengthwise**
**1 onion - cut into 8 pieces**
**1 tbsp oil, 1 tsp ginger-garlic paste**
**2 tbsp hoisin sauce**
**1 tbsp soya sauce, 2 tbsp red chilli sauce**
**1 tsp cornflour mixed with ¼ cup water**
**¼ tsp salt, oil for frying**

**THIN COATING BATTER**
**½ cup cornflour, 2 tbsp plain flour**
**1 tsp ginger-garlic paste**
**½ tsp salt, ¼ tsp white pepper powder**
**1 tsp soya sauce, ½ tsp vinegar, 1 tsp lemon juice**
**¼ cup water to make the batter**

1. Wash and wipe dry bhindi with a clean napkin. Cut into 2 long pieces lengthwise.
2. Mix all ingredients of the batter in a big bowl, adding enough cold water (about ¼ to ½ cup) to get a coating batter of pouring consistency. Do not make the batter too thick or too thin.
3. Dip the bhindi in batter and mix well. The batter should coat the vegetable lightly. If not, sprinkle 2 tbsp more cornflour on the vegetable and mix well.
4. Deep fry in hot oil putting one piece at a time to get crisper bhindis. Do not pick up a handful of pieces to fry together. Add only that much quantity of bhindi which the kadhai can hold (fry in batches). Deep fry till pale golden on medium heat. Remove on paper napkin.
5. Heat 1 tbsp oil in a pan and stir fry onions for 2 minutes.
6. Add the ginger-garlic paste and saute for half a minute.
7. Shut off the flame, add the hoisin sauce, soya sauce, red chilli sauce and ¼ tsp salt. Mix well.
8. At serving time, return to fire and add the fried bhindi and the cornflour paste, mix gently for a minute. Serve immediately.

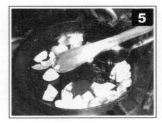

**Tip:** Hoisin sauce is available at all leading food stores. In absence of it you can use tomato ketchup.

# Cauliflower in Pepper Sauce

*Picture on page 120*                    *Serves 2-3*

**½ of a small cauliflower - cut into ¾" florets (1½ cups cut)**
**2 tbsp oil**
**a pinch of salt, ½ tsp pepper**
**pinch of ajinomoto (optional)**
**greens of 1 spring onion - cut into ½" pieces**

**SAUCE**
**1 white portion of spring onion - chopped**
**¼ tsp ginger paste**
**¼ tsp chopped garlic**
**6 peppercorns (saboot kali mirch)**
**1 tsp freshly ground black pepper (crush few saboot kali mirch to get fresh pepper)**
**½-1 tsp soya sauce, 1 tsp vinegar**
**¼- ½ tsp salt or to taste**
**a pinch of ajinomoto**
**2 tbsp oil**

**MIX TOGETHER**
**1½ cups water**
**1 vegetable seasoning cube (maggi or knorr)**

**PASTE**
**1¾ tbsp cornflour, ¼ cup water**

1.  Cut cauliflower cut into ¾" florets with a little stalk.
2.  Chop white portion of spring onion. Cut the green portion into ½" pieces.
3.  Crush 1 vegetable seasoning cubes and add with 1½ cups of water in a saucepan. Give one boil and keep aside.
4.  Mix cornflour with water to a smooth paste. Keep aside.
5.  Heat 2 tbsp oil in a wok or a kadhai and add cauliflower.
6.  Stir fry the cauliflower for 3-4 minutes on medium heat till brown specs appear on the cauliflower.
7.  Add a pinch of salt, ¼ pepper and pinch of ajinomoto. Keep aside.
8.  Heat 2 tbsp oil. Reduce heat and add white portion of spring onion, ginger paste, chopped garlic and peppercorns. Cook till garlic changes colour. Reduce heat, add black pepper, soya sauce, vinegar, salt and ajinomoto.
9.  Add water mixed with a seasoning cube. Give one boil.
10. Add the prepared cornflour paste. Cook till sauce thickens slightly.
11. Add fried cauliflower and greens of spring onion. Remove from fire. Serve hot.

# Steps of Cauliflower in Pepper Sauce

# Stir fried Snow Peas/Beans

*Picture on page 99*                    *Serves 4*

**200 gms snow peas or french beans**
**50-75 gm paneer - cut into thin, 2" long pieces**
**1 onion, 4 tbsp oil**
**1½" piece ginger - cut into juillenes or thin match sticks (1½ tbsp)**
**3-4 green chillies - shredded (cut into thin pieces lengthwise**

**OTHER INGREDIENTS**
**1½ tbsp soya sauce**
**2½ tbsp tomato ketchup**
**1 tbsp vinegar**
**1 tsp red chilli sauce**
**2 tbsp sherry or wine, optional**
**1½ tbsp worcester sauce**
**½ tsp salt, ¼ tsp pepper, or to taste**
**½ tsp ajinomoto (optional)**
**2 tbsp dry bread crumbs**

1.  Remove strings/threads from snow peas or beans. If using snow peas, keep whole. If using french beans, cut each into 1½-2" pieces. If using beans, boil 4-5 cups water with 1 tsp salt and 1 tsp sugar. Add beans and boil for 1-2 minutes. Strain.
2.  Peel onion. Cut into half and then cut widthwise to get half rings, which when opened become thin long strips and you get shredded onion.
3.  Heat 4 tbsp oil in pan. Add onion, cook till golden.
4.  Add ginger juillenes and green chillies. Stir fry for 1-2 minutes till ginger turns golden.
5.  Add snow peas or beans and stir fry for 3-4 minutes till vegetable turns crisp-tender. Keep the vegetable spread out in the pan while stir frying.
6.  Reduce heat. Add soya sauce, tomato ketchup, vinegar, red chilli sauce, sherry, worcester sauce, salt, pepper and ajinomoto.
7.  Add paneer and mix well.
8.  Add bread crumbs.Stir fry on low heat for 2 minutes till the vegetable blends well with the sauces. Serve hot.

# *Potato Strings in Hot Ginger Sauce*

*Serves 4*                    *Picture on cover*

**2 potatoes**
**capsicums - sliced very thinly to get jullienes (slice in same way as potatoes)**
**3½ tsp ginger paste**
**2 onions - chopped**
**1 tsp salt, ¾ tsp pepper**
**1 tsp soya sauce, 2 tsp tomato ketchup**
**2 vegetable seasoning cubes (maggi, knorr or any other)**
**2¼ tbsp cornflour mixed with ½ cup water**

1. To make stock with cube, Crush 2 vegetable seasoning cubes and add with 2 cups of water in a saucepan. Give one boil and keep aside.
2. Peel potatoes and cut each into thin slices, and cut further each slice into very thin fingers to get jullienes. Cut capsicum also in the same way to get thin fingers.
3. Heat oil in a kadhai and deep fry some shredded potatoes at a time. Fry in batches till golden brown and crisp. Drain on paper napkins. Repeat to fry the remaining potato strings.
4. Heat 4 tbsp oil in a kadhai. Add ginger paste. Cook on low flame for 1-2 minutes.
5. Add the chopped onion, cook till golden.
6. Add salt and pepper. Stir fry for a few seconds.
7. Add soya sauce, tomato ketchup and the prepared seasoning water or stock. Give one boil.
8. Add cornflour paste, cook till the sauce just starts to get thick. Remove from fire.
9. At serving time, add fried potatoes and capsicum. Mix well and serve hot immediately.

# Half Balls & Veggies in Sauce

*Picture on page 109*                    *Serves 4*

### BALLS
**2 cups cauliflower - grated finely**
**1 tsp soya sauce**
**½ tsp salt, ½ tsp pepper**
**2 tbsp cornflour**
**1 tsp ginger/garlic - chopped**
**2 bread slices - churned in a mixer to get fresh bread crumbs**

### SAUCE
**1 onion - cut into 8 pieces to get 1" squares**
**1 carrot - cut into thin slices lengthwise, cut each slice diagonally into 1" pieces**
**1 capsicum- cut into 1" square pieces**
**10-15 spinach leaves (paalak) - remove stem & keep whole**
**1 tsp garlic - finely chopped, 1 tsp chopped ginger**
**½ tsp soya sauce, 1 tsp tomato sauce**
**2 tsp green chilli sauce**
**1 green chilli - chopped**
**½ tsp vinegar ½ tsp salt, ¼ tsp pepper**
**¾ tsp sugar**
**3 tsp cornflour mixed with 2 cups water**

1. Mix all ingredients written under balls. Add fresh bread crumbs churned in a mixer. Mix well and make balls as you do for koftas.
2. Heat oil in a kadhai and deep fry the balls till golden brown.
3. Cut each ball into 2 from the middle and keep aside.
4. Cut carrot into thin slices lengthwise, cut each slice diagonally into 1" pieces.
5. Heat 2 tbsp oil in a pan. Add onion and cook till soft.
6. Add carrot, capsicum and spinach leaves without stem, saute for 2 minutes.
7. Add garlic, ginger, saute for ½ a minutes.
8. Remove from fire. Add soya sauce, tomato sauce, green chilli sauce, chopped green chilli, vinegar, salt, pepper and sugar. Return to fire. Cook sauces for a 10-15 seconds.
9. Add cornflour paste, cook for a few minutes till a thin sauce which coats the spoon is ready. Keep aside till serving time.
10. At serving time, add balls and heat thoroughly and serve immediately.

# Steps of Half Balls & Veggies in Sauce

# *Mongolian Lotus Stem*

*A sweet and sour lotus stem in a Chinese sauce.*

*Picture on facing page*                    *Serves 3-4*

**200 gm lotus stem (Bhein)**

**BATTER**
**4 tbsp cornflour, 4 tbsp plain flour (maida)**
**½ tsp salt, ¼ tsp pepper**
**2 flakes garlic - crushed to a paste, ¼ cup water**

**OTHER INGREDIENTS**
**2 cups vegetable stock (see page 37) or 2 cups water mixed with 2 vegetable seasoning cubes (maggi)**
**4 tbsp oil**
**3 spring onions - white part finely chopped & greens of onions cut into 1" pieces**
**10 flakes garlic - crushed**
**6 tbsp tomato ketchup, 1 tbsp vinegar**
**1 tsp salt or to taste, 1 tsp sugar**
**2 tbsp cornflour dissolved in ½ cup water**

1. Peel lotus stem & cut diagonally into paper thin slices. To parboil lotus stem, boil 4 cups water with 1 tsp salt. Add sliced lotus stem to boiling water. Boil for 2 minutes. Strain. Refresh in cold water. Strain, keep aside.
2. Mix all ingredients of the batter together.
3. Wipe dry the vegetable with a clean kitchen towel. Dip each piece in batter. Deep fry in two batches to a golden yellow colour. Do not brown them. Keep aside.

4. To make stock with cubes, mix 2 vegetable seasoning cubes with 2 cups of water in a saucepan. Crush cubes. Give one quick boil and keep aside.
5. In a frying pan heat 4 tbsp oil. Add the finely chopped white part of green onions.
6. Add garlic. Remove from fire.
7. Add tomato ketchup, vinegar, salt and sugar.
8. Add the prepared seasoning cube water or vegetable stock. Boil. Simmer for a minute.

9. Add dissolved cornflour to stock, stirring continuously till the sauce just starts to thicken. Keep aside till serving time.

10. At serving time, add the lotus stem and green part of spring onions and cook for 1-2 minutes. Serve hot.

# Tofu in Hot Garlic Sauce

*Serves 3-4*  *Picture on opposite page*

**200 gm tofu (paneer can be used instead)**

**BATTER**
**3 tbsp cornflour**
**3 tbsp plain flour (maida)**
**1 tsp Soya sauce**
**½ tsp garlic or ginger paste**
**¼ tsp each of pepper & salt**
**¼ tsp ajinomoto, optional**
**¼ cup water**

**GARLIC SAUCE**
**1 capsicum - cut into tiny cubes**
**3 tbsp oil**
**20 flakes garlic - chopped & crushed roughly in a small spice grinder (1½ tbsp)**
**2 dry, red chillies - broken into bits and deseeded**
**4 tbsp tomato ketchup**
**2 tsp red chilli sauce**
**2 tsp Soya sauce**
**½ tsp pepper, 1 tsp salt, a pinch sugar**
**2 tsp vinegar**
**¼ tsp ajinomoto (optional)**
**1½ cups water**
**2 tbsp cornflour mixed with ½ cup water**

1. To prepare the sauce, peel and grind the garlic to a very rough paste in a small grinder. Keep the mixer on just for 1-2 seconds. Do not make a smooth paste.
2. Heat oil. Remove from fire. Add garlic and red chilli bits. Stir till garlic starts to change its colour.
3. Add tomato ketchup, red chilli sauce, Soya sauce, pepper and salt. Return to fire and cook for 1 minute on low heat. Add sugar, vinegar and ajinomoto.
4. Add capsicum. Stir for 1-2 seconds to mix.
5. Add water, give one boil.
5. Add cornflour paste, stirring all the time. Cook for 2 minutes on low heat. Remove from heat. Keep sauce aside.
6. Cut tofu or paneer into 1" cubes.
7. Make a thick coating batter by mixing all ingredients with a little water.
8. Dip tofu or paneer pieces and deep fry to a golden colour. Keep aside.
9. At serving time, add fried tofu to sauce and boil for 2 minutes. Serve with rice.

◄ **Vegetable Fried Rice: Recipe on page 113, Tofu in Hot Garlic Sauce**

# Paneer Steak & Mung Beans

*Paneer steaks topped with a semi dry preparation of mung beans and some vegetables.*

*Picture on page 51*          *Serves 4-6*

**200 gms paneer or tofu (take a full block of paneer weighing 200 gms)**
**4 tbsp oil**
**2 flakes garlic - crushed**
**1 tsp grated ginger**
**1 onion - finely sliced**
**1 cup mung bean sprouts**
**½ cup snow peas or 6-8 French beans chopped into ¾" pieces**
**1 red or yellow capsicum - cut into 1" square pieces**
**2 tsp sugar**
**½ tsp salt**
**¼ tsp pepper**
**1 tbsp soya sauce**
**1 tsp cornflour blended with ¼ cup of water**

**BATTER**
**3 tbsp cornflour**
**3 tbsp plain flour (maida)**
**2 tbsp suji (semolina)**
**¼ cup ice cold water**
**2 tbsp chopped coriander**
**½ tsp salt**
**¼ tsp pepper**
**2 flakes garlic - crushed to a paste**

1.  Cut whole block of paneer lengthwise into big, flat 4 slices. Cut each slice further into 2 pieces from the middle to get 8 square or rectangular pieces of about 1½" width ¼" thickness.
2.  Mix all ingredients of the batter in a bowl. Add just enough water, to make a batter of a thick coating consistency, such that it coats the pieces of paneer.
3.  Heat 4 tbsp oil in a pan. Remove from fire & swirl pan (rotate by holding from the handle) to coat the whole bottom of the pan nicely with oil. Return to fire.
4.  Dip each paneer slice in the batter. Coat on all the sides. Fry in two batches in the pan till well browned and crisp on both sides. Remove from pan and keep aside till serving time.
5.  Heat the remaining oil in the pan. Add garlic and ginger and stir-fry for 1 minute.

*Contd...*

6. Add sliced onion and stir-fry till onion turns soft.
7. Add bean sprouts and beans or snow peas and yellow or red capsicum. Stir-fry for 1 minute.
8. Add sugar, ½ tsp salt, pepper. Add soy sauce and mix well. Cook for 2-3 minutes.
9. Add cornflour paste. Mix well for 1-2 minutes.
10. To serve, arrange the paneer steaks in a serving platter. Pour the moong beans with vegetables on the steak. Heat in a microwave and serve hot.

# *Vegetables in Ginger Garlic with Sesame Seeds*

*Serves 4*

### PARBOILED VEGETABLES
**1 small carrot - parboiled & cut into round slices**
**¼ of a small cauliflower or broccoli - cut into small flat florets and parboiled**

### OTHER VEGETABLES
**1 small onion - cut into 4 pieces and separated**
**1 capsicum - cut into ½" cubes**
**4-5 button mushrooms or dried mushrooms**
**50 gm cabbage - cut into 1" squares**
**4-6 baby corns - keep whole**

### SAUCE
**1 tbsp ginger paste,  6-8 flakes garlic - crushed**
**2 tbsp tomato ketchup**
**1 tsp soya sauce, 2 tsp vinegar**
**½ tsp white pepper,  ½ tsp salt, or to taste**
**¼ tsp sugar**
**1½ tbsp cornflour mixed with 1 cup water**
**1 tbsp sesame seeds (til)**

1. To parboil vegetables, boil 4 cups water with ½ tsp salt. Peel the carrot and drop the whole carrot and cauliflower florets in boiling water. Let them boil for 2 minutes. Remove from water. Cut carrots into ¼" thick round slices.
2. Cut capsicum into ½" pieces. Trim mushrooms, cut onions into fours and separate the slices. Cut cabbage into 1" squares. Keep baby corns whole.
3. Dissolve cornflour in 1 cup water and keep aside.
4. Heat 1½ tbsp oil in a kadhai. Reduce heat and add ginger paste and ½ of crushed garlic. Fry till changes colour.
5. Except capsicum, add all the other vegetables. Stir for 4-5 minutes. Add capsicum. Add salt and pepper. Mix and remove the vegetables. Keep aside.
6. For sauce- In the same kadhai heat 1 tbsp oil. Add sesame seeds, wait till golden. Add the left over garlic, stir till it changes colour. Reduce heat.
7. Add tomato ketchup, soya sauce, vinegar, white pepper, salt and sugar. Mix.
8. Add cornflour paste and cook stirring continuously till sauce turns thick.
8. At serving time mix in stir fried vegetables and serve immediately. Serve sprinkled with 1 tsp of toasted sesame seeds.

**Note:** Toast sesame seeds on a tawa (griddle) till golden.

# Billy Kee Mushroom in Sauce

*Serves 4*

**1 packet mushrooms (200 gms)**

**BATTER**
**4 tbsp cornflour, 4 tbsp plain flour (maida)**
**2 tbsp tomato ketchup**
**2 tbsp chopped coriander**
**½ tsp salt, ¼ tsp pepper, 2 flakes garlic - crushed to a paste**

**OTHER INGREDIENTS**
**1½ tbsp almonds (badam)**
**1 tbsp chopped garlic, 1 tbsp chopped ginger, 1 green chilli - chopped**
**3 spring onions - chop greens and white separately**
**1 cup tomato puree, 1 tbsp soya sauce**
**½ tsp red wine, optional, 1 tbsp red chilli sauce**
**1 tsp salt, ¼ tsp ajinomoto**
**1¼ tsp sugar, 1½ cups water**
**2 tbsp cornflour mixed with ¼ cup water**

1. Mix all ingredients of the batter in a bowl. Add just enough water, about 4-5 tbsp, to make a batter of a thick coating consistency, such that it coats the mushrooms.
2. Wash and wipe dry the mushrooms with a clean kitchen towel.
3. Heat 4 tbsp oil in a pan. Remove pan from fire. Swirl the pan (rotate) to coat the bottom of the pan nicely with oil. Return to fire.
4. Dip mushrooms in batter. Pan fry in two batches till crisp brown. Keep aside.
5. Heat the remaining oil in the a pan or wok, add almonds and stir for a minute. Remove from oil and keep aside.
6. Add garlic, ginger and green chilli. Stir for a minute.
7. Add chopped white part of spring onions & cook till soft.
8. Add tomato puree. Mix. Reduce heat. Add soya sauce, red wine, red chilli sauce, salt, ajinomoto and sugar. Stir till it leaves oil.
9. Add ½ of spring onion greens and 1½ cups water. Boil. Simmer for 2-3 minutes.
10. Add the fried mushrooms and fried almonds.
11. Dissolve cornflour in ¼ cup of water and add to the mushrooms. Thicken the sauce a little, stirring continuously. Garnish with the remaining spring onions greens and serve hot.

# Broccoli in Garlic Butter Sauce

*Broccoli cooked in a cream sauce with almonds sprinkled on top.*

*Picture on page 2*　　　　　　　　*Serves 4*

**250 gm (1 medium head) broccoli**
**½ tsp salt**
**½ tsp sugar**
**1 tbsp coriander- chopped**

**SAUCE**
**¾ cup vegetable stock or 1 veg seasoning cube (maggi or knorr)**
**3 tbsp butter**
**1 onion - sliced**
**15 flakes garlic - crushed to a paste (1 tbsp)**
**1 tbap chopped coriander**
**3 tbsp flour (maida)**
**1 cup milk**
**2 tsp mustard paste (optional)**
**½ tsp pepper**
**¾ tsp salt, or to taste**
**1 cup thin cream (if the cream is thick, then thin it down with ¼ cup milk and then measure to get 1 cup thin cream)**

**TO SPRINKLE**
**2 tbsp almonds - chopped**

1. To make stock with cube, boil 1 cup water with 1 vegetable seasoning cube. Give one boil and remove from fire. Keep aside.
2. Cut broccoli into medium sized florets with long stalks.
3. Boil 5 cups of water in a large pan. Add 2 tsp salt and 1 tsp sugar to the water. Add broccoli pieces to the boiling water. Bring to a boil. Keep boiling for 2 min. Drain. Refresh in cold water. Wipe broccoli well with a clean kitchen towel.
4. In a heavy bottom pan put 3 tbsp butter. Keep on fire and add sliced onions and cook till soft. Add garlic paste. Cook till garlic changes colour.
5. Add boiled broccoli and coriander, stir fry for 2 minutes.
6. Add maida. Stir for 1 minute on medium flame till light golden.
7. Reduce heat. Add milk, stirring continuously.
8. Add prepared stock, mustard paste, pepper and salt. Cook stirring, on low flame till sauce thickens. Remove from fire.
9. Add cream. Keep aside till serving time.
10. At serving time, heat sauce on low heat, serve garnished with chopped almonds.

# Steps of Broccoli in Garlic Butter Sauce

# Vegetable HongKong with Fried Noodles

*Picture on facing page*                    Serves 4

**3-4 medium florets of cauliflower - parboiled**
**1 carrot - cut into leaves (see page 55) - parboil the carrot leaves**
**5-6 french beans - parboiled**
**2-3 leaves of cabbage - torn into big pieces, 1 capsicum - cut into big pieces**
**1 spring onion - quartered**
**3 tbsp oil**
**2-3 tbsp walnuts (akhrot) or cashewnuts (kaju)**
**1 tsp finely chopped garlic or ginger**
**2-3 dry red chillies - broken into pieces**
**a pinch ajinomoto (optional)**
**2 tbsp soya sauce, 2 tsp vinegar, 2 tsp chilli sauce**
**salt and pepper to taste, ½ tsp sugar**
**1½ tbsp cornflour dissolved in 1 cup water**

### FRIED NOODLES
**2 cups boiled noodles (see pg 103), 2 tbsp oil, ½ tsp salt, ¼ tsp ajinomoto (optional)**
**¼ tsp red chilli powder, 1 tbsp soya sauce**

1. To parboil vegetables, boil 4 cups water with ½ tsp salt. Drop cauliflower florets, carrot pieces and beans in boiling water. Let them boil for 1-2 minutes. Remove from fire. Strain and refresh with tap water

2. Heat 3 tbsp oil in a wok or a frying pan. Reduce heat. Add walnuts or cashewnuts. Fry to a golden colour on low flame. Remove from pan.

3. Add ginger or garlic to the oil. Cook for ½ minute.

4. Add red chillies, all the parboiled vegetables, cabbage, capsicum and onion.

5. Add ajinomoto. Stir fry for 2 minutes. Add soya sauce, vinegar, chilli sauce, salt, pepper and sugar.

6. Add cornflour paste, stirring continuously. Cook till the sauce thickens and coats the vegetables. Keep aside.

7. To prepare the fried noodles, heat 2 tbsp oil in a clean wok. Reduce heat. Add salt, ajinomoto and chilli powder. Mix. Add soya sauce and stir for a few seconds. Add boiled noodles. Fry turning occasionally, till the noodles are evenly browned.

8. Add more soya sauce if a darker colour is desired. Remove from fire.

9. To serve, place the vegetables in the centre of a plate and surround them with fried noodles. Garnish the vegetables with fried nuts.

# Kung Pao Corn

*Vegetables in a delicious red sauce with corn.*

*Serves 3-4*          *Picture on opposite page*

**1 cup tinned corn kernels**
**1 capsicum - sliced thinly**
**2 tbsp cashewnuts (kaju)**
**2 tbsp oil**
**3 dry, red chillies - keep whole**
**1 onion - chopped**
**1 tbsp ginger - chopped, 1 tbsp garlic - chopped**
**2 tomatoes - pureed in a mixer**
**1 tsp soya sauce, 1 tsp red chilli sauce, ½ tsp white vinegar**
**¼ tsp sugar, ¼ tsp salt or to taste**

**MIX TOGETHER**
**2 tsp cornflour, 2 cups water**
**1 vegetable seasoning cube (maggi)**

1. Mix together cornflour, water and seasoning cube. Crush seasoning cube with your hands before mixing it to the water. Mix everything well and keep aside.
2. Slice/slit the kaju from the middle into 2 pieces.
3. Heat the oil, add the kaju. Saute until kaju turn golden brown. Remove kaju from oil and keep aside.
4. In the same pan add 1 tbsp oil, reduce heat add dry red chillies, saute for a minute. Do not let them turn black.
5. Add onion and cook till golden.
6. Add the chopped ginger and garlic and saute for a few more seconds.
7. Add pureed tomatoes, soya sauce, red chilli sauce, vinegar, sugar and salt. Cook for about 3-4 minutes till tomatoes turn dry
8. Add corn. Mix well.
9. Stir the above prepared cornflour- cube mixture with a spoon. Add it to the pan. Give one boil. Remove from fire. Keep aside till serving time.
10. At serving time, add the capsicum and the fried kaju. Mix well. Serve.

# Schzewan Vegetables

*Garnish these vegetables in hot sauce with deep-fried rice noodles if you like.*

*Serves 3-4*

**1 medium sized onion - cut into 8 pieces**
**1 medium sized carrot - cut into thin rounds**
**8 french beans - cut into 1" pieces**
**5 babycorns - cut diagonally into 2 pieces**
**¼ of a small cucumber (kheera)- cut into round slices and halved**
**1 capsicum - cut into 8 pieces**
**2 tbsp oil**

**MIX TOGETHER**
**1 tbsp oil**
**2 dry red chillies - break into very small pieces and remove seeds**
**¼ tsp chilli powder**
**3 laung (cloves) - crushed**
**8 flakes garlic - crushed**
**3 tbsp vinegar**
**2 tsp sugar**
**2 tsp soya sauce**
**2 tsp tomato ketchup**
**½ tsp salt, ¼ tsp pepper**
**1 tsp sherry or rice wine (optional)**
**2 cups stock (page 37) or 2 cups water mixed with 1 veg seasoning cube**
**3 tsp cornflour**

**GARNISH**
**¼ cup rice seviyaan or glass (rice) noodles**

1. Cut all the vegetables and keep aside.
2. Mix in a bowl, all the ingredients written under mix together. Keep aside.
3. Heat oil in a kadhai, add onion and cook till soft.
4. Add carrot, beans and babycorn. Cook for 2-3 minutes till crisp tender.
5. Add cucumber and capsicum, saute for few seconds.
6. Add the prepared sauce mixture. Boil. Cook for 1-2 minutes on low flame till sauce thickens slightly and vegetables turn crisp-tender. Remove from fire.
7. For garnishing, heat oil in a kadhai for deep frying. Add few rice seviyaan. Fry for a minute. Remove on napkin and keep in an air tight box till further use.
8. At serving time, add vegetables to the sauce and heat thoroughly. Serve garnished with few deep fried noodles or seviyaan.

# Steps of Schzewan Vegetables

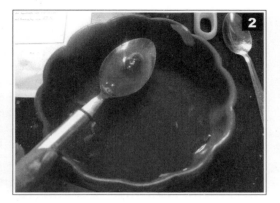

# Cubed Paneer & Veg Sizzler

*Serves 2*

**100 gms paneer - cut into ½" cubes**
**6 mushrooms - each cut into four pieces**
**1 small onion - cut into 4 pieces and separated**
**1 carrot - cut into small cubes**
**½ capsicum - cut into ½" pieces,**
**1 slice of tinned pineapple - cut into small pieces**
**½ tsp salt and ½ tsp freshly crushed pepper, or to taste**
**2 tbsp oil**

**SAUCE**
**2 tbsp oil**
**6-7 flakes garlic - crushed**
**2 green chillies - deseeded & chopped finely**
**½ tbsp soya sauce, a few drops tabasco or capsico sauce**
**1 tbsp red chilli sauce**
**3 tbsp tomato ketchup**
**1 tbsp vinegar, ¼ tsp pepper and ½ tsp salt, or to taste**
**2 level tbsp cornflour dissolved in 1½ cups water**

**TO SERVE**
**2 tbsp butter**
**a sizzler plate, rice boiled with salt and lemon juice**

1. Heat 2 tbsp oil in a non-stick pan or kadhai. Add mushrooms. Saute till light brown. Add onion and carrots. Saute for 2-3 minutes till carrots are crisp-tender.
2. Add capsicum, pineapple and paneer. Add salt and freshly crushed pepper. Cook for 1 minute. Remove all vegetables and paneer from the kadhai and keep aside.
3. To prepare the sauce, heat 2 tbsp oil in a clean kadhai. Reduce heat. Add garlic and green chillies. Stir for a few seconds on low heat till garlic just changes colour.
4. Remove from fire. Add soya sauce, a few drops tabasco or capsico sauce, red chilli sauce, tomato ketchup and vinegar. Cook on slow fire for a few seconds. Add salt and pepper to taste. Add cornflour paste, stirring continuously till a sauce is ready. Add vegetables and paneer. Cook for 1 minute on low heat.
5. To serve, remove the iron sizzler plate from the wooden base. Heat the iron plate by keeping it directly on the flame. Reduce heat and let the iron plate be on fire while it is being filled. Put 2-3 tbsp water in the wooden base and scatter 1 tbsp butter cut into pieces on the wooden base. Keep wooden base aside.
6. When the iron plate is heated, scatter 1 tbsp butter here and there. Place

2-3 cabbage leaves on the iron plate and arrange rice on it. Leave on slow flame for 2 minutes for the rice to get heated. Put the hot vegetables in sauce in the centre portion of the rice. When the hot sauce falls on the hot plate, it sizzles. With the help of a firm pair of tongs (sansi), place the iron plate on the on the wooden tray. Serve sizzling hot.

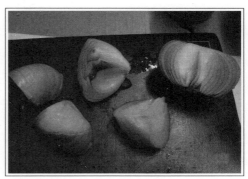

*Cutting of mushrooms and onions*

# The Chinese Sizzler

*Hot ginger or garlic sauce is poured over stir fried vegetables placed on a hot iron plate. Noodle cutlets and french fries accompany the vegetables.*

*Serves 4*

### NOODLE CUTLETS
**3 boiled potatoes - grated**
**1 onion - chopped finely**
**1 carrot - cut into tiny cubes**
**1 capsicum - cut into tiny cubes**
**1 tsp salt, ½ tsp red chilli powder**
**1 tsp soya sauce, 2 tbsp oil**
**6 tbsp bread crumbs**

### COATING
**2 tbsp plain flour (maida) mixed with ¼ cup water**
**1 cup boiled noodles**

1. Heat oil. Add onion and carrot and stir fry for 1-2 minutes. Add capsicum. Stir fry for ½ minute.
2. Add potatoes, soya sauce, salt and red chilli powder. Mix well.
3. Remove from fire. Add bread crumbs. Mix well and shape into 4 oval balls. Flatten them slightly.
4. Dip in a thin batter prepared by mixing 2 tbsp plain flour with ¼ cup water.
5. Cover with boiled noodles. Deep fry to a golden brown colour. Keep the noodle cutlets aside.

### GINGER SAUCE
**2 dry, red chillies, 2" piece ginger**
**2 tbsp oil**
**1 tsp soya sauce, 2 tbsp tomato ketchup**
**1 tbsp vinegar**
**¼ tsp ajinomoto (optional), ½ tsp each of salt and pepper, or to taste**
**1 cup water**
**1½ tbsp cornflour dissolved in ½ cup water**

1. Grind red chillies with ginger to a paste.
2. Heat oil. Add ginger-red chilli paste, stir fry on low flame for 1 minute.
3. Add soya sauce, tomato ketchup, vinegar, ajinomoto, salt and pepper. Cook for 1 minute.
4. Add water. Boil. Add cornflour paste, stirring continuously. Cook till thick.

### STIR FRIED VEGETABLES
**1 onion - cut into fours & separated**
**2 cabbage leaves - torn into big pieces**
**¼ of a small cauliflower - cut into florets**
**5-6 french beans - cut into 1" long pieces**
**1 carrot - cut into leaves & flowers**
**salt and pepper to taste**
**¼ tsp ajinomoto (optional)**
**a pinch of sugar**
**2 tbsp oil**

1. To parboil vegetables, boil 4 cups water with 1 tsp salt. Add cauliflower, carrots and french beans in boiling water. Let it boil for just 1 minute. Remove from water. Strain and refresh in cold water
2. Heat oil. Add onions.
3. Stir fry for 1 minute. Add cabbage. Stir for 1 minute.
4. Add all other parboiled vegetables, salt, pepper, ajinomoto and sugar. Stir fry for a few seconds. Remove from fire.

### TO SERVE
**a few cabbage leaves**
**50 gm chilled butter - cut into ¼" cubes**
**juice of 1 lemon**
**a few potato fingers**

1. To serve, remove the iron plate from the wooden stand. Heat the iron plate on high flame, till very hot. Place it back on the wooden stand.
2. Place 2 halves of a cabbage leaf on a hot iron plate fitted on a wooden stand. Push a few tiny cubes of ice cold butter sprinkled with lemon juice under the leaves.
3. Arrange the noodle cutlets and stir fried vegetables on the cabbage leaves.
4. Pour the prepared hot sauce over it.
5. Fried potato fingers may accompany the sizzler.

# Babycorn Aniseed

*Dry babycorns fragrantly flavoured with fennel, can be served as a side dish or a snack.*

*Picture on facing page*                    Serves 4

**200 gm babycorns**

**BATTER**
**3 tbsp cornflour, 2 tbsp plain flour (maida)**
**2 tbsp suji (semolina)**
**1 tbsp saunf (aniseeds or fennel) - powdered**
**½ tsp soya sauce, ½ tsp garlic or ginger paste**
**½ tsp salt, ¼ tsp ajinomoto, optional**
**¼ cup water, approx.**

**RED CHILLI - GARLIC PASTE**
**3-4 flakes garlic, 2 dry red chillies - broken into bits and deseeded**
**1 tsp saunf (fennel)**

**OTHER INGREDIENTS**
**2 spring onions - chop white and cut greens separately into ¼" pieces diagonally**
**¾ tsp salt, ¼ tsp ajinomoto**
**1 tbsp soya sauce, 2 tbsp tomato sauce, ½ tbsp vinegar**
**2 tsp cornflour mixed with ½ cup water**

1. Cut a thin slice from the end (not the pointed end) from each baby corn. Wash and wipe well on a clean kitchen towel.
2. Make a thick coating batter by mixing all ingredients of batter with a little water.
3. For the red chilli - garlic paste, soak all ingredients together in ¼ cup water for 10 minutes and grind to a paste along with the water.
4. Heat 3 tbsp oil in a pan. Remove pan from fire and swirl or rotate the pan so as to coat the bottom of the pan nicely with oil. Return to fire.
5. Dip babycorn in the prepared batter and shallow fry half of the babycorns in a pan on medium flame, turning sides, till golden and cooked. Remove on paper napkins and keep aside.
6. Heat the remaining oil in the pan. Add white of spring onions. Cook for a minute.
7. Add the prepared red chilli- garlic paste. Stir for a minute.
8. Add ¼ cup water. Stir.
9. Reduce heat. Add salt, ajinomoto, soya sauce, tomato sauce and vinegar.
10. Add cornflour paste. Stir for a minute till thick. Add greens of onions and babycorns. Mix well and serve hot.

# Honey Chilli Veggies

Serves 4          *Picture on opposite page*

**1 small carrot - parboiled and cut into round slices**
**1 capsicum - cut into ½" cubes**
**½ cup cauliflower or broccoli - cut into small, flat florets (¼ of a small flower)**
**1 small onion - cut into 4 pieces and separated**
**4-5 mushrooms**
**4-6 baby corns (optional)**
**¼ tsp freshly ground pepper, 1 tsp salt, or to taste**
**a pinch ajinomoto (optional)**
**2-3 tbsp oil**
**3-4 dried, red chillies - broken into small pieces**
**8-10 flakes garlic - crushed**
**2 tsp chilli sauce, 1½ tbsp tomato sauce, 1 tbsp soya sauce**
**2 tsp honey**
**½ tbsp vinegar**
**3 tbsp cornflour mixed with ¼ cup water**

1. To parboil carrot, boil 4 cups water with 1 tsp salt. Peel the carrot and drop the whole carrot in boiling water. Let it boil for 2-3 minutes. Remove from water. Cut carrots into ¼" thick round slices or flowers.

2. Cut capsicum into ½" pieces. Break cauliflower or broccoli into small florets and cut each floret into two. Trim mushrooms and baby corns, keeping them whole. Cut onion into fours and separate the slices.

3. Dissolve cornflour in ¼ cup water and keep aside.

4. Heat oil in a kadhai. Reduce heat and add broken red chillies and garlic.

5. Stir and add baby corns, carrots, cauliflower, onion and mushrooms. Stir for 4-5 minutes. Add capsicum. Add pepper, salt and ajinomoto..

6. Stir and add chilli sauce, tomato sauce, soya sauce, honey and vinegar. Pour 2 cups of water and bring to a boil. Lower heat and simmer for ½ minute.

7. Add the dissolved cornflour and cook till the vegetables get done and the sauce turns thick.

8. Spread the warm rice in a serving plate. Pour the hot vegetables over the rice and serve immediately.

◁ *Vegetable Manchurian: Recipe on page 57*
◁ *Haka Noodles with Vegetables: Recipe on page 104*
◁ *Honey Chilli Veggies*

# Shredded Aubergine in Sweet & Sour Sauce

*Serves 6*

**1 round big aubergine (baingan bharte waala) - peel & cut into ½" thick slices, cut slices into ¾" broad fingers (long, thick pieces)**

**TOMATO STOCK**
**2 onions - chopped**
**4 big tomatoes - chopped**
**7-8 flakes garlic - crushed**
**¾" piece ginger - chopped**
**3 cups of water**

**OTHER INGREDIENTS**
**3 tbsp oil, 3 onions**
**2 dry, red chillies - broken into bits**
**½ tsp white or black pepper**
**1½ tsp salt or to taste, ¼ tsp ajinomoto**
**2 tbsp tomato ketchup, 1 tsp vinegar**
**½ tsp sugar, ½ tsp soya sauce**
**4 tbsp cornflour mixed with ¼ cup water**

1. Peel baingan and cut into ½" thick slices. Cut slices into ¾" broad fingers. Sprinkle ½ tsp salt on them and keep aside for 20 minutes.
2. Cut each onions into four pieces.
3. For sauce, pressure cook all ingredients for the tomato stock together to give 2-3 whistles.
4. Remove from fire after the pressure drops down. Strain.
5. Keep the tomato stock aside.
6. Heat 3 tbsp oil in a pan. Stir fry onions till soft.
7. Add red chilli pieces, pepper, salt and ajinomoto.
8. Add prepared tomato stock. Give one boil. Reduce the flame.
9. Add tomato ketchup, vinegar, sugar and soya sauce. Boil.
10. Add cornflour mixed with ¼ cup water, stirring continuously.
11. Simmer for 1-2 minutes till thick.
12. Heat oil in a kadhai. Deep fry baingan till tender. Drain on napkin. Keep aside.
13. At the time of serving, add fried aubergine fingers and heat for a minute.

# Garlic Honey Cottage Cheese

### Serves 3-4

**100 gms cottage cheese (paneer) - cut into 1" cubes and deep fried**
**a 3-4" piece of cabbage - cut into 1½" squares (1 cup)**
**1 small onion - cut into 4 pieces and separated**
**½ tsp freshly ground pepper, ½ tsp salt, or to taste**
**2 tsp red chilli sauce, 1 tbsp tomato sauce**
**1 tbsp soya sauce**
**2 tsp honey**
**½ tbsp vinegar**
**3 tbsp cornflour mixed with ¼ cup water**
**2-3 tbsp oil**

### GRIND TOGETHER
**4 dry red chillies - -remove seeds, break into small pieces & soak in water**
**for 10 minutes**
**12-15 flakes garlic**
**1 tsp vinegar**
**¼ tsp jeera (cumin), 2-3 saboot kali mirch (peppercorns)**

1. Soak dry red chillies. Drain and grind to a paste with garlic, vinegar, jeera and saboot kali mirch. Keep aside.
2. Cut cabbage into 1½" square pieces. Cut onion into fours & separate the slices.
3. Dissolve cornflour in ¼ cup water and keep aside.
4. Heat oil in a kadhai. Reduce heat and add red chilli and garlic paste.
5. Stir & add onion. Mix. Add cabbage. Stir for 3-4 minutes. Add pepper and salt.
6. Stir. Reduce heat. Add chilli sauce, tomato sauce, soya sauce, honey and vinegar.
7. Add paneer and mix well for 2 minutes.
8. Pour 1½ cups of water and bring to a boil. Lower heat.
9. Add the dissolved cornflour and cook till the sauce turns thick. Serve hot.

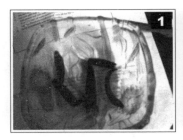

# Moons in Almond Sauce

*Picture on page 100*                    *Serves 4*

**2 cucumbers (kheera)**
**6-8 almonds (badam)**

**ALMOND SAUCE**
**2 tbsp oil**
**15 almonds (badaam) - ground to a paste with ¼ cup water**
**1" piece ginger - crushed to a paste (1 tsp)**
**5-6 flakes garlic - crushed (1 tsp)**
**2 green chillies - chopped**
**½ onion - very finely chopped**
**1 tbsp soya sauce**
**1½ tbsp tomato ketchup**
**2 tsp vinegar**
**½ tsp salt**
**¼ tsp pepper**
**½ bread slice - ground in a mixer to get fresh crumbs**

1. Remove bitterness of the cucumber. Peel. Cut lengthwise into two halves. With the help of a scooper or the back of a teaspoon, remove the seeds from the cucumber by pulling the spoon straight down the length of the cucumber half. This way you get a groove in the cucumber piece.
2. Cut the cucumber into ½" thick, half-moon slices.
3. Heat 1 tbsp oil in a pan. Add almonds, stir fry for 2-3 minutes till well fried. Remove from pan.
4. In the remaining oil, add cucumber moons (pieces) & stir fry for a minute. Sprinkle a pinch of red chilli powder and some salt. Remove from pan and keep aside.
5. Finely chop the fried almonds.
6. To prepare almond sauce, heat 2 tbsp oil. Reduce heat. Add ginger and garlic. Fry on low flame for 1 minute.
7. Add green chillies and onions. Cook till they turn light brown.
8. Reduce heat and add soya sauce, tomato ketchup, vinegar, salt and pepper. Cook for 1-2 minutes.
9. Add 1½ cups of water. Boil. Keep on slow fire for 2-3 minutes.
10. Add almond paste and fresh bread crumbs. Cook till slightly thick. Keep sauce aside.
11. To serve, boil the sauce. Add the fried cucumber moons (pieces) and the chopped almonds to the sauce. Add ½ tsp more of soya sauce if you like. Keep on slow fire for one minute till heated thoroughly.

# Steps of Moons in Almond Sauce

# Sweet & Sour Vegetables

*Serves 4*

**TOMATO STOCK**
1 onion - chopped
2 big tomatoes - chopped, 4-5 flakes garlic - crushed
½" piece ginger
1½ cups water

**OTHER INGREDIENTS**
3 tbsp oil
2 small onions - cut into four pieces
4-5 medium florets of cauliflower - parboiled
1 carrot - parboiled
10 french beans - parboiled
¼ of a small cucumber (kheera)
1 small capsicum - cut into 1" pieces
½ tsp salt to taste
½ tsp white pepper, ¼ tsp ajinomoto
¼ cup tomato ketchup, 2-3 tbsp vinegar
2 tsp sugar, 2 tsp soya sauce
2 tbsp cornflour

1. Pressure cook all ingredients for the tomato stock together to give 2-3 whistles.
2. Remove from fire. Strain after the pressure drops. Keep tomato stock aside.
3. Scrape carrot, string french beans.
4. Boil 2-3 cups water with 1 tsp salt. Drop whole carrot, whole french beans and cauliflower florets in the boiling water for one minute. Strain. Cool.
5. Cut beans and carrots diagonally, beans into 1" long pieces and carrots into ¼" thick round slices. Keep aside.
6. Heat 3 tbsp oil. Stir fry onions and cauliflower for 2 minutes.
7. Add parboiled carrot, french beans, kheera and capsicum.
8. Add salt, pepper and ajinomoto. Stir fry vegetables for 2 minutes.
9. Add the prepared tomato stock.
10. Add tomato ketchup, vinegar, sugar and soya sauce. Boil.
11. Add cornflour mixed with ½ cup water, stirring continuously.
12. Simmer for 2 minutes till thick. Serve hot with fried rice or noodles.

# Cantonese Vegetables

*Serves 8*

**2 medium sized carrots - parboiled & cut into ¼" thick rounds**
**½ cabbage - cut into 1½" square pieces**
**2 medium sized onions - cut into fours**
**1 capsicum - cut into 8 pieces**
**1 small cucumber - cut into rounds**
**2 tbsp soya sauce**
**1 tbsp chilli sauce**
**1 tbsp vinegar**
**1 tsp pepper, ¼ tsp ajinomoto (optional), 1 tsp sugar**
**2 cups water mixed with 2 seasoning cubes**
**salt to taste**
**3 tbsp cornflour dissolved in ¼ cup water**

1. To parboil carrot, boil 4 cups water with 1 tsp salt. Peel the carrot and drop the whole carrot in boiling water. Let it boil for 2 minutes. Remove from water. Cut carrots into ¼" thick round slices or flowers.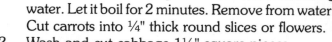
2. Wash and cut cabbage 1½" square pieces.
3. Stir fry each vegetable separately in little oil.
4. Do not over fry. The colour of the vegetables should not change.
5. Take out the vegetables into a serving dish.
6. Heat 1 tbsp oil. Add soya sauce, chilli sauce, vinegar, pepper, ajinomoto and sugar. Stir on low heat for a few seconds.
7. Add water. Boil. Add salt to taste
8. Add cornflour paste, stirring continuously. Remove from fire when thick.
9. Add the vegetables to the sauce and serve hot.

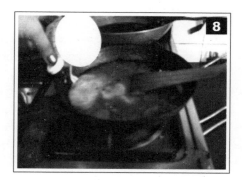

# Nutty Paneer with Broccoli

*A dry dish with the crunch of cashews.*

*Serves 4*

**1 small flower of broccoli (150 gms) - cut into small (1") florets with very little stem**
**250 gms paneer - cut into 1" cubes**
**1 large onion - cut into 1" pieces**
**1 large tomato - cut into 4 pieces, remove pulp and cut into 1" pieces**
**5-6 roasted kajus (cashewnuts) or regular kajus roasted on a tawa**
**3 tbsp oil**
**6-7 flakes garlic - crushed and chopped**
**2 green chillies - chopped finely**
**1 tbsp soya sauce**
**a dash of tabasco or capsico sauce**
**1 tbsp chilli garlic sauce, 1 tbsp tomato ketchup**
**½ tsp salt, or to taste, ½ tsp pepper**

1. Roast kaju on a tawa till it changes colour.
2. Heat 1½ tbsp oil in a non-stick pan or a kadhai.
3. Add onion. Cook till soft.
4. Add broccoli, cook for 2 minutes.
5. Add paneer. Cook for 1 minute.
6. Remove pulp of tomato pieces and add to the paneer. Saute for a few seconds.
7. Remove all vegetables and paneer from the kadhai and keep aside.
8. Heat 1½ tbsp oil in a clean kadhai. Add crushed garlic and green chillies.
9. Reduce heat. Add soya sauce, tabasco or capsico sauce, chilli garlic sauce, tomato ketchup. Cook on slow fire for a few seconds.
10. Add the cooked vegetables and paneer.
11. Add salt and pepper to taste.
12. Cook for 2-3 minutes on low heat, sprinkling water occasionally, if required, till the sauces coat the paneer and vegetables.
13. Serve hot sprinkled with roasted kajus.

*Stir Fried Snow Peas/Beans: Recipe on page 64* ➤

# Stir Fried Red & Green Cabbage

*Serves 4*

**1 small green cabbage - shredded**
**½ of a small red cabbage - shredded**
**1 capsicum - shredded (optional)**
**3-4 green chillies - shredded**
**3 tbsp oil**
**½ tsp salt**
**½ tsp pepper, or to taste**
**½ tsp ajinomoto (optional)**
**¼ tsp crushed dry red chillies**

**MIX TOGETHER IN A CUP**
**½ cup water**
**1½ tbsp cornflour**
**1½-2 tbsp soya sauce**
**2½-3 tbsp tomato ketchup**
**2 tbsp vinegar**

1. Mix together all the ingredients written under mix together in a cup. Keep aside.
2. Shred green, red cabbage and capsicum into thin strips or slices/fingers.
3. Heat oil in a big kadhai. Add both cabbages, capsicum and green chillies. Stir fry for 2-3 minutes on high flame.
4. Add salt, pepper, ajinomoto and red chilles.
5. Add all the ingredients which have been mixed together in a cup. Stir fry on low heat for 2-3 minutes till the vegetable is almost dry, but not completely dry.
6. Serve hot, sprinkled with crushed red chillies.

**Stir Fried Red & Green Cabbage**

◁ *Moons in Almond Sauce: Recipe on page 94*

# RICE & NOODLES

**Rice or noodles form the staple food of the Chinese. Short grained rice is preferred. For noodles, the nest like coiled noodles a preferred to the straight one. Always add noodles or rice to boiling water. When cooked, drain and cool before using. Rub oil over the noodles so that they don't stick to each other.**

Rice Noodles: These extremely thin noodles resemble long, transculent white hair. Rice noodles are just soaked in hot water for 10 minutes and then drained before use. When deep fried they explode dramatically into a tangle of airy, crunchy strands that are used for garnish.

Crispy Fried Noodles or Rice: Noodles or Rice are 90% cooked. They are removed from fire when almost done but not fully soft. These are dried on a muslin cloth. Small batches are put in a metal strainer and deep fried by putting the rice in the strainer in medium hot oil. These are fried till crisp and golden.

# Perfect Boiled Rice

## Serves 2

### 1½ cups uncooked rice, 2 tsp salt, 6 cups water

- To boil rice, clean and wash 1½ cups rice. Soak rice for 10 minutes.
- Boil 6 cups of water with 2 tsp salt. Add rice.
- Cook, uncovered, over a medium flame, stirring occasionally, until the rice is just tender but not **overcooked**.
- Drain the rice and let it stand in the strainer for sometime. Fluff with a fork. Spread on a tray and cool under a fan to separate the rice grains.
- About 4 cups of cooked rice is ready. The rice should be boiled **2-3 hours** before making fried rice. Hot rice when stir fried tends to get mushy.

**Note:** Parboiled, good quality rice (sela) should be used. Long grained rice is better. 1 cup uncooked rice will give about 2½ cups cooked rice.

# Perfect Boiled Noodles

## Serves 2-3

### 100 gm noodles, 6 cups water, 1 tsp salt, 2 tsp oil

- In a large pan, boil 6 cups water with 1 tsp salt and 1 tsp oil. Add noodles to boiling water.
- Cook uncovered, on high flame for about 2-3 minutes only.
- Remove from fire before they get **overcooked**. Drain.
- Wash with cold water several times.
- Strain. Leave them in the strainer for 15-20 minutes, turning them upside down, once after about 10 minutes to ensure complete drying. Apply 1 tsp oil on the noodles and spread in a tray till further use.

# Chinese Steamed Rice

## Serves 2-3

### 1 cup uncooked long grained rice, 2 cups water, 1 tsp salt, 1 tbsp refined oil

- Clean and wash rice thoroughly.
- Heat water with salt and oil. When it boils, add the rice.
- Slow down the fire, keep a griddle (tava) under the pan of rice & cook for about 15 minutes, until the water is absorbed and the rice is cooked.

# *Haka Noodles with Vegetables*

*Picture on page 90*                    *Serves 4*

## FRIED NOODLES
**100 gm noodles - boiled**
**2 tbsp oil**
**3 dry, whole red chillies - broken into bits**
**½ tsp chilli powder, ½ tsp salt, 2 tsp soya sauce**

## VEGETABLES
**3-4 flakes garlic - crushed and chopped (optional)**
**2-3 spring onions or 1 ordinary onion**
**3-4 tbsp bean sprouts - optional**
**2 tbsp shredded bamboo shoots - optional**
**1-2 tbsp dried mushrooms**
**1 carrot - shredded (cut into thin long matchsticks or grated)**
**½ cup shredded cabbage**
**1 capsicum - shredded**
**½ tsp ajinomoto (optional)**
**½ tsp each of salt & pepper, ½ tsp sugar**
**1 tbsp soya sauce, 2 tsp vinegar**
**1 cup water, 1½ tbsp cornflour dissolved in ½ cup water**

1. In a pan, heat 2 tbsp oil. Remove from fire, add broken red chillies and chilli powder.
2. Return to fire and mix in the boiled noodles. Sprinkle salt and soya sauce. Mix well. Stir fry for 1 minute, till evenly brown in colour.
3. Keep the fried noodles aside.
4. To prepare the vegetables, shred all vegetables.
5. Heat 3 tbsp oil. Reduce heat and add garlic.
6. Add vegetables in sequence of their tenderness - onions, sprouts, bamboo shoots, mushrooms, carrot, cabbage and capsicum.
7. Add ajinomoto, sugar, salt and pepper. Add soya sauce and vinegar. Cook for ½ minute.
8. Add water. Boil.
9. Add cornflour mixture, stirring continuously. Cook for 1 minute till thick. Remove from fire.
10. To serve, spread the fried noodles on a platter.
11. Pour the prepared hot vegetables over the noodles. Serve.

# Pepper Fried Rice

*Serves 3-4*

**1½ cups uncooked rice**
**5 saboot kali mirch (whole peppercorns)**
**3 flakes garlic - crushed & chopped (optional)**
**2 green chillies - chopped finely**
**2 green/spring onions - chopped till the greens**
**2 carrots - grated and squeezed well**
**1 tsp salt or to taste**
**1½ tsp freshly crushed peppercorns**
**½ tsp ajinomoto (optional)**
**½ tsp vinegar**

1. To boil rice, clean and wash 1½ cups rice. Soak rice for 10 minutes.
2. Boil 6 cups of water with 2 tsp salt. Add rice. Cook, uncovered, over a medium flame, stirring occasionally, until the rice is just tender but not **overcooked.** Drain the rice and let it stand in the strainer for sometime. Fluff with a fork. Spread on a tray and cool under a fan to separate the rice grains.
3. Chopped green /spring onions till the greens, keep greens and white separately.
4. Heat 3 tbsp oil in a pan/kadhai. Add saboot kali mirch, garlic, green chillies and white of onions. Cook for a minute.
5. Add grated carrot, salt, pepper and ajinomoto. Cook for ½ a minute.
6. Add rice and vinegar.
7. Add green onions. Stir fry the rice for 2 minutes. Serve hot.

# Pea Cinnamon Noodles

*Stir fried noodles with cinnamon, an excellent accompaniment to any wet dish.*

*Serves 4*

**200 gm noodles - boiled**
**3 tbsp oil**
**2-3 flakes of garlic - crushed**
**2 dry, whole red chillies - broken into pieces**
**½ tsp red chilli flakes or powder**
**1 tsp salt, or to taste, ¼ tsp pepper**
**3" piece cinnamon (dalchini) - powdered (1 tsp)**
**½ cup peas (matar)- boiled**

1. In a large pan, boil 6 cups water with 1 tsp salt and 1 tsp oil.
2. Add noodles to boiling water. Cook uncovered, on high flame for about 2 minutes only. Remove from fire before they get **overcooked.** Drain.
3. Wash with cold water several times. Strain. Leave them in the strainer for 15-20 minutes, turning them upside down, once after about 10 minutes to ensure complete drying. Apply 1 tsp oil on the noodles and spread on a tray. Keep aside till further use.
4. Heat 3 tbsp oil. Reduce heat. Add crushed garlic. Stir. Remove from fire.
5. Add broken red chillies, red chilli flakes or powder and peas. Return to fire and mix well.
6. Add the boiled noodles.
7. Sprinkle salt, pepper and cinnamon powder on the noodles. Mix well with the help of 2 forks. Fry for 2-3 minutes, till the noodles turn pale brown in colour. Serve.

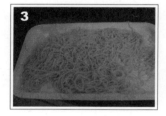

# Peanut Fried Rice

*Fried rice flavoured with peanuts.*

*Serves 3-4*

**1½ cups uncooked rice**
**3 tbsp oil**
**4 flakes garlic - crushed (optional)**
**2 green chillies - chopped finely**
**2 green onions - chopped till the greens, keep greens separate**
**1 tsp salt, 1 tsp pepper, ¼ tsp ainomoto (optional)**
**½ tsp soya sauce (according to the colour desired), 1 tsp vinegar (optional)**
**½ tsp tomato ketchup**

**GRIND TOGETHER TO A PASTE**
**3 tbsp roasted peanuts**
**5½ tbsp milk**

**FOR GARNISHING**
**2 tbsp roasted peanuts - roughly crushed on a chakla belan**

1. To boil rice, clean and wash 1½ cups rice. Soak rice for 10 minutes.
2. Boil 6 cups of water with 2 tsp salt. Add rice. Cook, uncovered, over a medium flame, stirring occasionally, until the rice is just tender but not **overcooked.** Drain the rice and let it stand in the strainer for sometime. Fluff with a fork. Spread on a tray and cool under a fan to separate the rice grains.

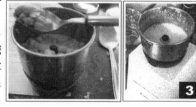

3. Grind all ingredients of paste to a smooth paste.
4. Chop spring onions till the greens, keep white and green separately.
5. Heat oil. Stir fry garlic, green chillies and white of onions.
6. Add peanut paste. Mix. Reduce heat, add salt, pepper and ajinomoto, soya sauce, vinegar and tomato ketchup. Mix.
7. Add boiled rice and green portion of spring onions. Mix and stir fry the rice for 2 minutes with the help of 2 forks. Remove from fire.
8. Serve hot garnished with crushed roasted peanuts.

# Chilli Garlic Noodles

*Stir fried plain noodles, which will be an excellent accompaniment to any sauce.*

*Serves 4*

**CHILLI NOODLES**
**100 gm noodles - boiled**
**3 tbsp oil**
**1 tsp garlic paste**
**3 dry, whole red chillies - broken into bits**
**½ tsp red chilli flakes or powder**
**½ tsp salt or to taste**
**½-1 tsp soya sauce**

1. In a large pan, boil 6 cups water with 1 tsp salt and 1 tsp oil.
2. Add noodles to boiling water. Cook uncovered, on high flame for about 2-3 minutes only. Remove from fire before they get **overcooked.** Drain.
3. Wash with cold water several times. Strain. Leave them in the strainer for 15-20 minutes, turning them upside down, once after about 10 minutes to ensure complete drying.
4. Apply 1 tsp oil on the noodles and spread in a tray, till further use.
5. Heat 3 tbsp oil. Add garlic paste, cook till golden.
6. Remove from fire, add broken red chillies and red chilli flakes or powder.
7. Return to fire and mix in the boiled noodles. Add salt and a little soya sauce. Do not add too much soya sauce.
8. Mix well with the help of 2 forks. Fry for 2-3 minutes, till the noodles turn a pale brown. Serve hot.

*Half Balls & Veggies in Sauce : Recipe on page 66*  ➤

# *American Chopsuey with Vegetables*

*Serves 4*        *Picture on opposite page*

**1 carrot**
**8 french beans**
**1 green chilli - shredded**
**1 capsicum - shredded, 1 onion - shredded**
**¾ cup cabbage - shredded**
**½ cup bean sprouts**
**¼ tsp ajinomoto (optional)**
**5 tbsp oil**
**½ tsp white pepper, salt to taste**
**1 tsp soya sauce, 1 tsp vinegar**
**4 tbsp tomato ketchup**
**2 cups water**
**3 tbsp cornflour dissolved in ½ cup water**

**CRISPY NOODLES**
**100 gms noodles - boiled, spread on a tray and sprinkled with 2-3 tbsp maida**
**oil for deep frying**

1. To prepare crispy noodles, deep fry the noodles in two batches, in hot smoking oil until crisp and golden brown. Keep aside.
2. Scrape carrot, string french beans.
3. Parboil them by dropping the whole carrot and french beans in 2 cups of boiling water with ½ tsp salt. Strain after half a minute. Cool.
4. Shred all vegetables (cut into thin long pieces) - capsicum, onion, cabbage, carrot and french beans.
5. Heat 5 tbsp of oil. Add sprouts and ajinomoto. Stir fry for 1 minute.
6. Add carrot, french beans, green chilli, capsicum, onion, cabbage, pepper and salt. Stir fry for 2 minutes.
7. Add soya sauce, vinegar and tomato ketchup. Cook for ½ minute.
8. Add water. Bring to a boil.
9. Add cornflour paste, stirring continuously. Cook for about 2 minutes, till thick. Keep aside.
10. To serve, spread crispy noodles on a serving platter, keeping aside a few for the top.
11. Top with the prepared vegetables.
12. Sprinkle some left over crispy noodles on it. Serve hot.

# Fried Noodles with Peas & Bean Sprouts

*Serves 3-4*

**100 gm noodles - boiled**
**3 tbsp oil**
**2 spring onions - chopped finely with the greens, keep greens separately**
**½ cup bean sprouts**
**2 capsicums - sliced finely**
**½ cup boiled peas (matar)**
**2 tbsp soya sauce**
**1 tbsp vinegar**
**½ tsp salt or to taste**
**¼ tsp pepper or to taste**
**a pinch of ajinomoto (optional)**

1. In a large pan, boil 6 cups water with 1 tsp salt and 1 tsp oil.
2. Add noodles to boiling water. Cook uncovered, on high flame for about 2-3 minutes only. Remove from fire before they get **overcooked.** Drain.
3. Wash with cold water several times. Strain. Leave them in the strainer for 15-20 minutes, turning them upside down, once after about 10 minutes to ensure complete drying. Apply 1 tsp oil on the noodles and keep aside till further use.
4. Heat 1 tbsp oil. Add the boiled noodles and fry for 1 minute till golden. Remove and keep aside.
5. Heat 2 tbsp oil in the same kadhai or pan. Add the white of spring onions and peas. Stir fry for ½ minute.
6. Add bean sprouts and capsicum. Stir fry for 1 minute.
7. Add the noodles. Sprinkle soya sauce, vinegar, salt, pepper and ajinomoto.
8. Toss well with 2 forks so that all the ingredients are mixed well. Check salt.
9. Transfer on to a serving dish and serve hot.

# *Vegetable Fried Rice*

*Serves 4*　　　　　　　*Picture on page 70*

**1½ cups uncooked rice - boiled and spread on a tray to dry**
**2 flakes garlic - crushed (optional)**
**2 green chillies - chopped finely**
**2 green onions - chopped till the greens, keep greens separate**
**¼ cup very finely sliced french beans**
**1 carrot - finely diced (cut into tiny cubes)**
**½ big capsicum - diced (cut into tiny cubes)**
**1 tsp salt**
**½ tsp pepper**
**¼ tsp ajinomoto (optional)**
**1-2 tsp soya sauce (according to the colour desired)**
**1 tsp vinegar (optional)**

1.　To boil rice, clean and wash 1½ cups rice. Soak rice for 10 minutes. Boil 6 cups of water with 2 tsp salt. Add rice. Cook, uncovered, over a medium flame, stirring occasionally, until the rice is just tender but not **overcooked.** Drain the rice and let it stand in the strainer for sometime. Fluff with a fork. Spread on a tray and cool under a fan to separate the rice grains.
2.　Heat 2 tbsp oil. Reduce heat. Add garlic, green chillies and white of onions. Stir.
3.　Add beans, stir for a minute.
4.　Add carrots. Stir fry for 1 minute.
5.　Add capsicum. Stir to mix.
6.　Add salt, pepper and ajinomoto. Mix well.
7.　Add rice. Reduce heat. Sprinkle soya sauce and vinegar on the rice.
8.　Mix well using 2 forks. Add greens of onions. Stir fry rice for 2 minutes. Serve.

# Chinese Chop Suey

*Serves 4*

**CRISPY NOODLES**
**100 gms noodles - boiled**
**1 tbsp flour (maida), oil for frying**

**OTHER INGREDIENTS**
**1 carrot - parboiled, 8 french beans - parboiled, ½ cup small florets of cauliflower**
**¾ cup shredded cabbage**
**1 capsicum - shredded**
**2 spring onions - cut white portion into 4 pieces and green into 1" pieces**
**½ cup bean sprouts**
**¼ tsp ajinomoto (optional), 1 tsp white pepper, 1 tsp sugar**
**1½ tbsp soya sauce, salt to taste**
**2½ tbsp cornflour mixed with 1/3 cup of water**

1. In a large pan, boil 6 cups water with 1 tsp salt and 1 tsp oil. Add noodles to boiling water. Cook uncovered, on high flame for about 2-3 minutes only. Remove from fire before they get **overcooked.** Drain. Wash with cold water several times. Strain. Leave them in the strainer for 15-20 minutes, turning them upside down, once after about 10 min to ensure complete drying. Apply 1 tsp oil on the noodles.
2. Sprinkle flour on noodles to discard any water present.
3. Heat about 2 cups of oil. Add half of the noodles. Stir, turning sides till noodles are golden in colour and form a nest like appearance. Remove from oil.
4. Drain on absorbent paper. Fry the left over noodles in the same way.
5. Scrape the carrot, string the french beans, remove the seeds from the capsicum and peel the onions.
6. To parboil vegetables, drop the whole carrot, french beans and cauliflower florets into 2 cups of boiling water to which ½ tsp salt has been added. Boil for 1 minute, drain and cool. Shred beans diagonally and carrots into match sticks.
7. Shred capsicum and quarter the onions.
8. Heat 5 tbsp oil in an iron pan and add white of spring onions, bean sprouts and ajinomoto fry over a high flame for 2 minutes. Add green of spring onions.
9. Add remaining vegetables, pepper, sugar & salt. Stir fry on high flame for 2 min.
10. Add soya sauce. Cook for ½ minute. Add water. Bring to a boil and add cornflour mixed with 1/3 cup water, stirring all the time, until thickened. Remove from fire.
11. To serve, put the crispy noodles at the bottom of a serving bowl and top with the vegetable mixture. Alternatively, serve crispy noodles and vegetable mixture side by side in a dish.

# Glass Noodles with Sesame Paste

*Glass noodles are thin long translucent noodles. In the absence of these the regular noodles or rice seviyaan can be used. Boil the regular noodles for 2 minutes where as the glass noodles or the rice seviyaan just needs to be soaked in hot water for 5 minutes.*

*Serves 6*        *Picture on page 21*

**100 gms glass noodles or rice seviyaan**
**2 tbsp oil**
**3 spring onions - cut into rings, till the greens, keep white separate**

**SESAME PASTE (GRIND ALL TOGETHER)**
**3 tbsp sesame seeds (til) - soak for 10 minutes in 5 tbsp hot milk & 2 tbsp water and then grind to a paste**
**½ tsp red chilli powder or to taste, ¾ tsp salt**
**4 flakes garlic - finely chopped**
**1½ tbsp soya sauce**
**½ tsp sugar**

1. Cut white spring onion into rings till the greens.
2. In a large pan, boil 8 cups water with 1 tsp salt & 1 tsp oil. Remove from fire. Add noodles to hot water. Cover & keep aside for 5 minutes in hot water. Drain.
3. Wash with cold water several times. Strain. Leave them in the strainer for 15-20 minutes, turning them upside down, once after about 10 minutes to ensure complete drying. Apply 1 tsp oil on the noodles and spread on a large tray. Dry the noodles under a fan for 15-20 minutes. Keep aside till further use.
4. Grind all ingredients of sesame paste to a smooth paste.
5. Heat oil in a pan, remove from fire. Swirl the pan to coat the bottom of the pan nicely with oil. Add white portion of spring onions, stir for a minute.
6. Add prepared sesame paste mixture, mix well and stir for 2 minutes on low heat.
7. Add boiled noodles, mix well. Add spring onion greens. Mix & remove from fire.

# Fried Rice with
# Babycorn & Bamboo Shoots

*Serves 4*

**1½ cups uncooked rice - boiled and spread on a tray to dry**
**6 cups water**
**3 tbsp oil**
**4 spring onions - chop green and white portion separately**
**½ cup chopped babycorns**
**½ cup sliced bamboo shoots**
**¼ tsp ajinomoto (optional)**
**salt to taste**
**2-3 tbsp soya sauce**

1. To boil rice, clean and wash 1½ cups rice. Soak rice for 10 minutes.
2. Boil 6 cups of water with 2 tsp salt. Add rice. Cook, uncovered, over a medium flame, stirring occasionally, until the rice is just tender but not **overcooked.** Drain the rice and let it stand in the strainer for sometime. Fluff with a fork. Spread on a tray and cool under a fan to separate the rice grains.
3. Peel the onions and cut the white into thin rings. Cut the greens also into thin slices.
4. Heat oil. Add white part of spring onions and babycorn. Cook on low heat for 2-3 minutes.
5. Add bamboo shoots, ajinomoto and salt over high flame for 1-2 minutes.
6. Add the rice, soya sauce and spring onion greens.
7. Stir fry over a high flame for 2 to 3 minutes. Serve hot.

# Vegetable Party Fried Rice

*Serves 4*

**1½ cups uncooked long grain rice**
**6 cups water**
**4 tbsp oil**
**1 tomato - chopped**
**¼ cup sliced mushrooms (optional)**
**¼ cup carrot - diced**
**¼ cup parboiled french beans - diced**
**¼ cup diced capsicum**
**¼ cup shelled green peas - boiled**
**1 cup finely chopped white portion of spring onions**
**¼ tsp ajinomoto (optional)**
**salt to taste**
**2 tbsp soya sauce**
**2 tbsp pineapple cubes (tinned pineapple)**
**1 tbsp fried almonds (badam)**
**1 tbsp fried walnuts (akhrot)**

1. To boil rice, clean and wash 1½ cups rice. Soak rice for 10 minutes.
2. Boil 6 cups of water with 2 tsp salt. Add rice. Cook, uncovered, over a medium flame, stirring occasionally, until the rice is just tender but not **overcooked**. Drain the rice and let it stand in the strainer for sometime. Fluff with a fork. Spread on a tray and cool under a fan to separate the rice grains.
3. Peel and chop onions finely.
4. Heat oil and add chopped tomato, fry for 2-3 minutes.
5. Add mushrooms and stir fry the mushrooms, over a high flame for 2 minutes.
6. Add all the vegetables, except onion tops and peas. Add ajinomoto and salt.
7. Add the rice, soya sauce, spring onion tops and green peas.
8. Stir fry over a high flame for 3 to 5 minutes.
9. Garnish rice with pineapple cubes, fried almonds, and walnuts.

# *Glutinous Rice*

*A sticky rice dish! It's a little sweet because of the honey added to it.*

*Serves 6*

**1½ cups uncooked rice (ordinary quality short grained rice, permal chaawal)**
**2 tbsp oil**
**1 onion - sliced**
**2 flakes garlic - crushed**
**2 spring onions - chop white and green part separately**
**2 green chillies - chopped**
**½ cup peas (matar)**
**½ tsp jeera powder (cumin powder), ½ tsp dhania powder (ground coriander)**
**1 tsp saunf - crushed**
**1 tsp salt, ½ tsp pepper**

**MIX TOGETHER**
**3 cups veg stock or 3 cups of water mixed with 1 vegetable seasoning cube**
**2 tbsp honey**
**2 tbsp soya sauce**

1. Wash and soak rice. Keep aside.
2. Mix all the ingredients written under mix together in a bowl. Keep aside.
3. Heat oil in a large deep pan, add sliced onion & garlic and stir-fry for 4-5 minutes or until onion is soft.
4. Add white part of spring onion, green chillies and peas.
5. Add jeera powder, dhania powder, crushed saunf, salt and pepper. Stir-fry for 1 minute.
6. Drain rice and add to the pan. Stir for 3-4 minutes on low heat.
7. Add stock-honey mixture and green of spring onion. Stir and bring to a boil.
8. Reduce heat and cook covered for 10 minutes or until rice is done and the water gets absorbed. Serve hot.

Final Dish

**Toffee Apples: Recipe on page 125** ➤

# Vegetable Chow Mein

*Serves 4*

**100 gm noodles**
**2-3 flakes garlic - crushed (optional)**
**1 onion - sliced**
**1 carrot - shredded**
**1 cup shredded cabbage**
**1 capsicum - shredded**
**¾ tsp salt, 1 tsp white pepper**
**a pinch sugar**
**¼ tsp ajinomoto (optional)**
**2 tsp soya sauce, 1 tbsp vinegar**
**1½ tsp chilli sauce**

1. In a large pan, boil 6 cups water with 1 tsp salt and 1 tsp oil.
2. Add noodles to boiling water. Cook uncovered, on high flame for about 2-3 minutes only. Remove from fire before they get **overcooked**. Drain.
3. Wash with cold water several times. Strain. Leave them in the strainer for 15-20 minutes, turning them upside down, once after about 10 minutes to ensure complete drying. Apply 1 tsp oil on the noodles and spread them on a tray.
4. Shred all vegetables into thin long strips. To shred onions, peel and cut into half. Cut each half into thin semi circles to get thin long strips of onion. To shred carrots, grate on the thick side of the grater.
5. Heat oil. Add sliced onion. Stir fry for 1- 2 minutes. Add garlic. Mix.
6. Stir fry carrots for ½ minute. Add cabbage and capsicum. Mix.
7. Add salt, pepper, sugar and ajinomoto. Mix.
8. Add boiled noodles. Sprinkle soya sauce and mix well with 2 forks so that all the ingredients are mixed well. Check salt. .
9. Add vinegar and chilli sauce. Stir fry for 1 minute. Add more soya sauce for a darker colour. Serve.

◁  *Cauliflower in Pepper Sauce: Recipe on page 62*

# DESSERTS

## Steps of Honey Crispies

Fettucine Pasta

1

4

5

# *Honey Crispies*

*Serves 6-8* *Picture on page 129*

**CRISPY FRIED NOODLES**
**100 gm flat noodles or flat pasta (fettuccine) - break into 4"- 5" length**
**1 cup maida, 1 tbsp oil**
**oil for frying**

**CARAMEL HONEY COATING**
**7 tbsp sugar, 2 tbsp oil**
**3 tbsp honey**
**3 tbsp sesame (til) seeds**

**TO SERVE**
**vanilla ice-cream**

1. Boil 6-8 cups water. Add noodles to boiling water and stir with a fork. Boil for 1-2 minutes till slightly soft. Do not over boil. Drain. Wash with cold water and strain. Keep in the strainer for 15 minutes for all the water to drain out. Sprinkle 1 tbsp oil and mix. Spread a muslin cloth on a large tray. Put the noodles on the cloth. Keep under the fan to dry out, for about 30 minutes.
2. Sprinkle 4-5 tbsp maida on the noodles. Leave them spread out on the tray.
3. Heat oil in a kadhai for frying.
4. Take ¼ quantity of noodles on a plate. Sprinkle 2-3 tbsp more maida on the noodles.
5. Use plate to put noodles in the kadhai, and not hands. Fry on medium heat, separating the noodles while putting them into the hot oil. Fry till light golden. brown.Keep aside.
6. For the caramel-honey coating, in a big kadhai put sugar with oil and heat over a slow flame, stirring till sugar dissolves.
7. When the sugar melts, add 1½ tbsp honey and sesame seeds. Stir till sesame seeds and sugar turns golden. Remove from fire.

8. Add the noodles and stir to mix well till coated with the caramel-honey coating. Pour 1½ tbsp more honey and mix well. Remove noodles from kadhai and store in an air tight container till further use.
9. Serve warm or at room temperature with ice cream.

# Date & Coconut Pancakes

*Serves 4*

**1 tbsp sesame seeds (til)**
**½ cup cornflour**
**½ cup plain flour (maida)**
**½ cup milk**
**½ cup water**
**2 tsp melted butter or oil**
**a pinch salt**
**oil for frying**

**FILLING**
**½ cup grated fresh coconut**
**½ cup dates - deseeded and finely chopped**
**¼ cup powdered sugar**

**TO SERVE**
**vanilla ice-cream**

1. Mix all ingredients of the filling together and keep aside.
2. Mix the cornflour, plain flour, milk, water, butter and salt into a thin pouring batter of a smooth consistency. Add sesame seeds and mix well. Add a little more water if the mixture appears a little thick.
3. Put 1 tsp oil onto a nonstick frying pan of about 7" diameter and keep on fire.
4. Do not make the pan too hot. Pour 1 small karchhi, (about 2 tbsp) of the batter in the pan and shake the pan in a circular motion so as to spread the batter evenly.
5. Cook firstly on one side until done and then on the other side.
6. Repeat with the remaining batter.
7. To serve, spread 1 tbsp of the filling on each pancake and fold. If desired, seal the edges by applying a little of the pancake mixture.
8. Fry until crisp. Cut into pieces and serve with vanilla ice cream.

# Toffee Apples

*Serves 4*

*Picture on page 119*

**3 delicious golden or red apples
oil for deep frying**

**CARAMEL COATING
1 cup sugar, 2 tbsp oil
2 tsp sesame (til) seeds
½ cup water**

**BATTER
½ cup plain flour (maida)
2 tbsp cornflour, ½ tsp baking powder**

1. Put the sugar, 2 tbsp oil and ½ cup of water in a pan and cook on a high flame.
2. When the mixture begins to bubble, stir continuously to prevent the sugar from burning.
3. Continue stirring the pan until the syrup is light brown in colour and feels sticky when felt between the thumb and the fore finger. It forms a thread when the finger is pulled apart.
4. Remove from the heat, add the sesame seeds and mix well. Keep the caramel syrup aside.
5. Mix the plain flour, cornflour and baking powder in a bowl. Add about ½ cup water to get a smooth, thick batter of a coating consistency.
6. Peel and cut the apples into four pieces. Remove the seeds. Cut each piece further into 2 pieces if the apples are big.
7. Heat oil for frying. Coat the apple pieces evenly with the batter and deep fry 5-6 pieces together at one time, in hot oil until golden.
8. Keep a serving bowl filled with ice-cubes ready and cover with water.
9. Put the fried apples in the caramel syrup and coat evenly.
   Drain well and dip immediately into the ice-cubes bowl.
   Keep for a few minutes till the caramel coating hardens.
10. Drain thoroughly. Keep aside till serving time.
11. Serve plain or with ice cream.

**Note:** You can use pears too instead of apples.

# Assorted Fruit Fritters

*Serves 8-10*

**1 large, firm mango - peeled**
**4 firm bananas - peeled**
**2 apples - peeled**
**4 slices pineapple**
**4-6 tbsp flour for dusting**
**¼ tsp cinnamon powder (dalchini powder)**
**oil for deep frying**

**TO SPRINKLE**
**½ tsp cinnamon powder (dalchini powdered)**
**icing sugar**

**BATTER**
**2 cups plain flour (maida)**
**1 tsp baking powder**
**¼ tsp salt**
**¾ cup milk**
**¾ cup cold water**

1.  Cut fruits into serving pieces.
2.  Combine flour and cinnamon and lightly dust fruits with it.
3.  To make the batter, sift plain flour. Mix flour, baking powder and salt into a bowl.
4.  Combine milk and water and beat into flour to form a smooth batter of a thick coating consistency. Add a little more water if required. Stir well before using.
5.  Dip fruit into batter and deep fry in hot oil until golden. Drain well.
6.  Arrange on a serving platter. Sift with the help of a sieve (channi) icing sugar. Then on top of icing sugar sprinkle cinnamom powder.

# Almond Float

*Serves 4*

**2½ cups milk**
**¼ cup sugar**
**2 drops almond essence**
**2 tbsp gelatine**
**½ cup water**
**some fresh fruits and canned lychees**

1. Keep milk in a pan and put on fire. When it is about to boil, remove from heat.
2. Add sugar. Cool slightly and then add almond essence.
3. Sprinkle gelatine over ½ cup water and leave until water is absorbed. Dissolve gelatine over low heat, stirring continuously. Stir gelatine into milk mixture.
4. Set the milk mixture in an aluminium tray or a cake tin in the refrigerator for 2-3 hours to set.
5. To serve, cut almond gelatine into diamond shapes. Place fruit in a serving bowl and arrange diamond shapes on top.

# Date & Sesame Wontons

*Serves 8-10*

**WONTONS WRAPPERS**
2 cups plain flour (maida), 1 tsp powdered sugar
oil for deep frying

**STUFFING**
¼ cup sesame seeds (til)
¼ cup brown sugar , ¾ cup chopped dates (khajoor)
1 tbsp butter - softened

**OTHER INGREDIENTS**
2 tbsp powdered sugar
oil for deep frying, 1-2 tbsp milk to seal
vanilla ice-cream to serve

1. To prepare the wonton wrappers, sieve the flour and sugar together.
2. Add ½ cup hot water gradually and make a soft dough. Knead well till smooth and cover and keep aside for 30 minutes.
3. Knead the dough with oiled hands until it becomes smooth and elastic. Keep dough aside.
4. Toast the sesame seeds on a medium flame until they are golden. Cool.
5. For the stuffing, mix toasted sesame seeds with brown sugar, dates and butter.
6. Divide the dough into 4 balls. Roll out each ball into thin chappatis.
7. Cut into 3½" square pieces. Place a little filling in the centre. Fold in half and press sides together by lifting one corner and joining to the opposite corner to make a triangle. Fold a little again, pressing firmly at both sides of the filling, but leaving corners open.
8. Bring 2 corners together, and cross over infront of the filling. Brush lightly with water where they meet, to make them stick.
9. Deep fry 5-6 pieces at a time in oil on low medium heat until golden. Cool.
10. Arrange in a platter. Sprinkle powdered sugar. Serve with vanilla ice-cream.

*Corn Rolls: Recipe on page 28* ➢
*Honey Crispies: Recipe on page 123* ➢

**CHINESE**
cooking for the Indian kitchen

**CONTINENTAL**
cooking for the Indian kitchen

**ITALIAN**
cooking for the Indian kitchen

**Low Calorie**
cooking for the Indian kitchen

**Tikka Seekh & Kebab**

**CONTINENTAL**
Non-Vegetarian

**MUGHLAI**
NonVeg Khaana

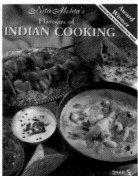

**Flavours of INDIAN COOKING**
(All Colour)

**LOW CALORIE RECIPES**

**The Best of CHICKEN**

**THAI COOKERY**

**PUNJABI NonVeg**

**Taste of KASHMIR**

**SNACKS NonVeg**

**The Best of MUTTON**

**BREAKFAST NonVeg**

**CHINESE COOKERY**

**MICROWAVE Cookery**

**MORE CHICKEN**

**ITALIAN NonVeg**

**OVEN Recipes NonVeg**

**Favourite NON-VEGETARIAN**

**Favourite Recipes**

# NITA MEHTA COOKERY CLASSES
## Starts 15ᵗʰ of Every Month (4 Day Course)

CALL TO REGISTER: 26214011, 26238727, 23250091, 23252948 (DELHI)